FASHION DOLL

DREAM CASTLE™

the Needlecraft™ Shop

ACKNOWLEDGEMENTS

For their generous contribution of supplies for designing this project, we wish to thank Darice® for providing plastic canvas, Nylon Plus™ yarn and metallic cord, and Uniek Crafts for providing Needloft™ metallic cord. Special thanks to Klaus Rothe of Sullivan Rothe Design, Berne, Indiana, Tom Buckley of JTM Colorscan, Ft. Worth, Texas, and Lori Powers of R.R. Donnelley & Sons Company, Chicago, Illinois.

ISBN: 0-9638031-3-1
Library of Congress Catalog Number: 93-86558
Printed in the United States of America.
First Printing: 1994

Dear Friend,

If you have ever had stars in your eyes and seen castles in the air, join us in making dreams come true for everyone who loves fashion dolls and fantasy. This castle is more than just another stitching project — it is the stage on which many new tales of adventure are about to unfold.

The castle is constructed in three sections that come apart for storage. Talented designer Diane T. Ray (get to know her on page 8) has created a solid structure and sturdy accessories that will hold up to years of play.

Almost everyone involved in this project here at The Needlecraft Shop has at one time or another been seen with his or her head buried deep inside one of the beautifully detailed castle rooms. Our editors and graphic artists took each and every stitch of the needle to heart when doing their parts in producing this book. And, our talented professional photographer and art director produced each color photo with an attention to stitch and embellishment detail.

We hope you enjoy following our "Show Me!" instructions. Rather than explaining things in dozens of words, we have included diagram after diagram showing exactly how the pieces are joined and in what order each piece should be handled. Instructions for the castle are written so that you will finish one section completely before moving on to the next.

To get the best results, carefully read the instructions on pages 10-13. Not only will beginners find all they need to get started, including stitch illustrations, but experienced stitchers will also get an overview of construction details that are special to this project.

We hope you enjoy the time you spend making Dream Castle dreams come true for someone in your life.

Janet

Janet Tipton

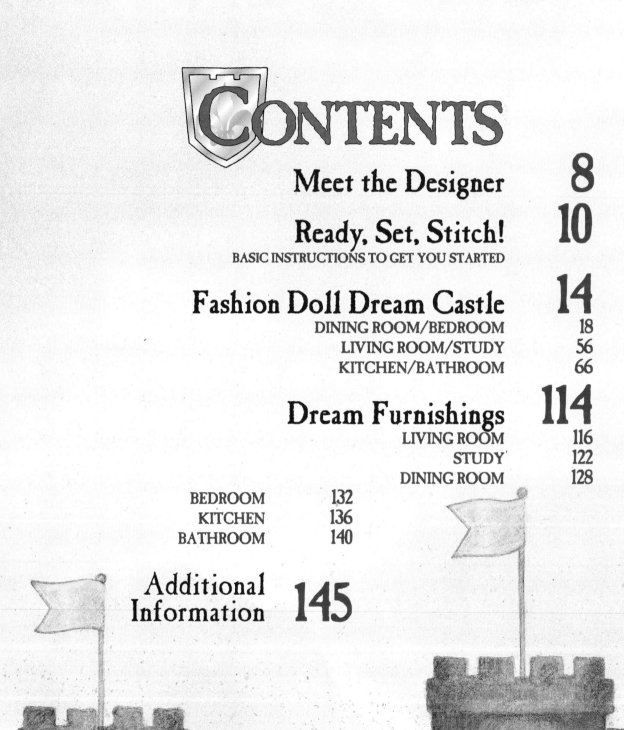

CONTENTS

FASHION DOLL

DREAM CASTLE™

PUBLISHER
Donna Robertson

EDITORIAL DIRECTOR
Carolyn Brooks Christmas

DESIGN DIRECTOR
Fran Rohus

CREATIVE DIRECTOR
Greg Smith

PRODUCTION DIRECTOR
Ange Workman

**EDITORIAL AND
GRAPHICS EDITOR**
Janet Tipton

COMPOSING EDITORS
Joni Sheedy, Jennifer Simcik

EDITORIAL TEAM
Kristine Hart, Susan Koellner

GRAPHIC ARTISTS
Derek Gentry, Pauline Rosenberger

GRAPHICS TEAM
Debby Keel, Sherman Klepfer,
Jessica Rice, Diane Simpson

EDITORIAL ASSISTANT
Janice Kellenberger

PUBLISHER'S ASSISTANT
Marianne Telesca

PROOFREADER
Mary Lingle

ART DIRECTOR
Rusty Lingle

PHOTOGRAPHER
Tammy Cromer-Campbell

ILLUSTRATIONS
Lois Sullivan

GRAPHIC ILLUSTRATIONS
Rusty Lingle

**ASSISTANT
PRODUCTION DIRECTOR**
Betty Gibbs-Radla

PRODUCTION MANAGER
Derek Gentry

**TECHNICAL DIRECTOR/
PRODUCTION**
John Nosal

TECHNICAL ASSISTANT
Jamie Hendry

DESIGN COORDINATOR
Brenda Wendling

PRESIDENT
Jerry Gentry

**VICE PRESIDENT
CUSTOMER SERVICE**
Karen Pierce

**VICE PRESIDENT
MARKETING**
Greg Deily

VICE PRESIDENT M.I.S.
John Trotter

eet the Designer

When castles started floating through the mind of designer Diane T. Ray in August of 1992, the fantasy world of fashion dolls was about to become a brighter place. Almost five feet long, this two-story plastic canvas dream home of princes and princesses was designed and constructed over a period of about six months.

An enthusiastic designer, Diane gained the experience required for the creation of such a giant project by establishing herself in 1992 with attention to accuracy and detail in the making of her *Fashion Doll Dream Home* furnishings series. The series of books includes a bedroom, living room, laundry room and bathroom.

Diane's projects are realistically engineered. For instance, during the design process of the living room furniture, Diane went to furniture stores to research the construction of sofas, chairs, tables and lamps. The result was a sturdy, construction-sound play set that holds up to hands-on use.

The same detailed accuracy found in the *Dream Home* series is reflected in her largest project to date — *Fashion Doll Dream Castle*. For the castle, Diane researched her subject at the library. She chose to furnish the structure with pieces dating from the 1600s – about as early in recorded history as you can find the kind of furnishings we've come to associate with medieval royalty. In spite of her diligence, Diane says she was not able to find a stove of the period to suit the regal lifestyles of her castle-dwelling dolls. But like a knight to the rescue, Diane designed the perfect stove from her imaginative sense of play.

Diane created her castle for children who love fashion dolls, but she hasn't forgotten things that will allow busy grown-ups to make the most of their stitching time. The end sections of this sturdy building are mirror images. And, before sweet dreams and princess visions fill your child's dreams at the end of a long evening of play, cleanup is easy — the castle's three sections come apart for storage.

Diane began actual construction of the project after a month of planning and used her dining room for her work area. With a table measuring three by four feet, the finished castle actually extended over the long ends of what normally would have been her family's eating table. Her husband, Rick, and her teenage sons, Mark and Todd, temporarily lost the use of their dining room.

"When I didn't want to move everything off the table and onto the narrow top of my sewing machine cabinet, I'd just send them into the living room to eat," Diane explained. During planning and construction of the castle, every available surface in the dining room — even the top of her china hutch — was filled with sheets of plastic canvas, skeins of yarn, pens, scissors and piles of papers for writing instructions as she worked.

Whereas prior to starting the castle she was accustomed to having several projects in the works at the same time, it seemed to Diane that the castle took up every waking moment. When she wasn't working on it, she was thinking about her next step. Sometimes she would awaken at 5 a.m. with new ideas. "Then in the afternoon I'd stop to get dinner going, then get right back to it," she said.

By February of 1993, the project was more than halfway to completion. Most of the castle's pieces were stitched and ready to assemble. The actual joining of pieces is what Diane looks forward to most in her designing process. "I get real excited. I want to see what it looks like, and I get in a hurry."

Diane's talents have surely bloomed since those days more than ten years ago when she and a long-time friend stitched on plastic canvas together and tinkered with designing practical things like purse pack tissue covers. But even now Diane must spend some of her time tossing aside miscut canvas and ripping out stitches. Backing up occasionally is part of the design process, because, she comments, "I've learned from my mistakes."

Diane says she was a tomboy while growing up and seldom played with dolls. When she did, her dolls wore clothes made by one of her aunts. And, she doesn't remember having any doll furniture to play with. Nowadays she finds herself enjoying the imaginative world of doll play as she creates projects, like the *Dream Castle*, that make dreams come true.

Diane lives with her family in Hobbs, New Mexico. Her husband, Rick, is the captain of a local firefighting crew. In their free time, Rick, Mark and Todd enjoy working together in the garage customizing their "sand rails," which are pipe-framed, two-seated vehicles similar to dune buggies. The boys' needlecrafting mom might still be a bit of a tomboy — she and the men in her life enjoy riding together over the sand dunes near their home.

eady, Set, Stitch!

Basic Instructions to Get You Started

Most plastic canvas stitchers love getting their projects organized before they even step out the door in search of supplies. A few moments of careful planning can make the creation of your *Dream Castle* even more fun.

First of all, prepare your work area. You will need a large, flat surface for cutting and construction, and you will need a place to store your materials. Good lighting is essential, and a comfortable chair will make your stitching time even more enjoyable.

Do you plan to make the castle and all the furnishings shown in the photos, or is building just the castle your goal? Will you buy supplies for the entire project all at once, or will you complete the castle before planning what you will need to make the furnishings?

Material lists for each of the above plans are included. Materials for the castle appear on page 14. Materials for each room of furnishings are listed separately at the beginning of each section. To purchase materials for all of the furnishings, see page 145; for materials for the entire set, castle and furnishings combined, see page 146. Whatever your plan, your shopping list, complete with check-off boxes, is ready.

Continental Stitch Illustration

Long Stitch Illustration
(over 3 bars)

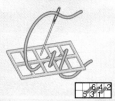

Whipstitch
(diagonally-cut canvas)

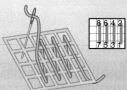

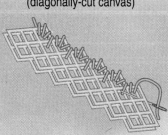

Dream Castle Supplies

Yarn, canvas, needles, cutters and most other supplies needed to complete the projects in this book are available through craft and needlework stores and mail-order catalogs. Other supplies are available at fabric, hardware and discount stores. For mail-order information, see page 13.

• *Needles & Other Stitching Tools*
A No. 16, blunt-end tapestry needle is used for stitching patterns on individual canvas pieces, for Overcasting and some Whipstitching. A curved upholstery needle will be needed for Whipstitching some of the walls of the castle. A small pair of embroidery scissors for snipping yarn is handy. Try using needle-nosed jewelry pliers for pulling the needle through several thicknesses of canvas and out of tight spots too small for your hand.

• *Canvas*
Seven-count plastic canvas is used throughout the castle. Large (12" x 18", 80 x 120 holes) sheets of stiff canvas are used for the walls and most furnishings. Standard-size (10⅝" x 13⅝", 70 x 90 holes) sheets of flexible and regular flexibility canvas as well as scraps of colored canvas are used for some accents. If a color is not specified in the materials list, you can assume clear canvas was used in the photographed model. Buy the same brand of canvas for each entire project. Different brands of canvas may differ slightly in the distance between each bar.

• *Marking and Counting Tools*
To avoid wasting canvas, careful cutting of each piece is important. For

some pieces with square corners, you might be comfortable cutting the canvas without marking it beforehand. But for pieces with lots of angles and cutouts, you may want to mark your canvas before cutting.

Always count before you mark and cut. To count holes on the graphs, look for the bolder lines showing each 10-hole section. These 10-count lines begin in the lower left-hand corner of each graph and are on the graphs to make counting easier. To count holes on the canvas, you can use your tapestry needle, a toothpick or a plastic hair roller pick. Insert the pick or needle slightly in each hole as you count. To count a large number of holes, use the 7-count ruler on page 13. Simply lay the edge of your canvas over the ruler, lining up the bars on the canvas with the markings on the ruler.

Most stitchers have tried a variety of marking tools and have settled on a favorite, which may be a crayon, permanent marker or grease pencil. One of the best marking tools is a fine-point overhead projection marker, available at office supply stores. The ink is dark and easy to see and washes off completely with water. After cutting and before stitching, it's important to remove all marks so they won't stain yarn as you stitch or show through stitches later. Cloth and paper toweling removes grease pencil and crayon marks, as do fabric softener sheets that have already been used in your dryer.

• *Cutting Tools*

When cutting long, straight sections, scissors, craft cutters or kitchen shears are the fastest and easiest to use. For cutting out detailed areas and trimming nubs, you may like using manicure scissors or nail clippers. If you prefer laying your canvas flat when cutting, try a craft knife and cutting surface — self-healing mats designed for sewing and kitchen cutting boards work well.

• *Yarn and Other Stitching Materials*

You may choose 2-ply nylon plastic canvas yarn (the color numbers of two popular brands are found in the general materials lists and Color Keys) or 4-ply worsted-weight yarn. There are about 42 yards per ounce of plastic canvas yarn and 50 yards per ounce of worsted-weight yarn.

Worsted-weight yarn is widely available and comes in wool, acrylic, cotton and blends. If you decide to use worsted-weight yarn, choose 100% acrylic for best coverage. Select worsted-weight yarn by color instead of the color names or numbers found in the Color Keys.

Plastic canvas yarn comes in about 60 colors and is a favorite of many plastic canvas designers. These yarns "wear" well both while stitching and in the finished project. When buying plastic canvas yarn, shop using the color names or numbers found in the Color Keys, or select colors of your choice.

Metallic cord is a tightly-woven cord that comes in dozens of glittering colors. For the castle you will need both solid metallic and mixed-color metallic cords. Though the sparkly look of metallics will add much to your project, you may substitute contrasting colors of yarn.

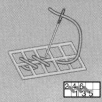

Reverse Continental Stitch Illustration

Overcast Stitch Illustration

Slanted Gobelin Stitch Illustration
(over 2 bars vertical)

Cutting Canvas for the Dream Castle

Follow all Cutting Instructions, Notes and labels above graphs to cut canvas. Each piece is labeled with a letter of the alphabet. Square-sided pieces are cut according to hole counts and some may not have a graph.

CONTINUED ON NEXT PAGE

Unlike sewing patterns, graphs are not designed to be used as actual patterns but rather as counting, cutting and stitching guides. Therefore, graphs may not be actual size. Count the holes on the graph, mark your canvas to match, then cut. The old carpenters' adage — "Measure twice, cut once" — is good advice. Trim off the nubs close to the bar, and trim all corners diagonally.

As you cut each piece, it is a good idea to label it with its letter and name. Use sticky labels, or fasten scrap paper notes through the canvas with a twist tie or a quick stitch with a scrap of yarn. Color coding of support pieces used in the base and inside the walls of the castle will make construction easier. Label and color code each piece in the same color as the graph using permanent marker or a knot of matching color yarn. To stay organized, you may want to store corresponding pieces together in zip-close bags.

If you accidentally cut or tear a bar or two on your canvas, don't worry! Boo-boos can usually be repaired in one of several ways: heat the tip of a metal skewer and melt the canvas back together; glue torn bars with a tiny drop of craft glue, super glue or hot glue; or reinforce the torn section with a separate piece of canvas placed at the back of your work. When reinforcing with extra canvas, stitch through both thicknesses.

Whipstitch Illustration

Slanted Gobelin Stitch Illustration
(over 2 bars horizontal)

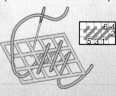

French Knot Stitch Illustration

Stitching the Canvas

Stitching Instructions for each section are found after the Cutting Instructions. First, refer to the illustrations of basic stitches found on pages 10-13 to familiarize yourself with the stitches used in the castle. Illustrations will be found near the graphs for pieces worked using special stitches. Follow the numbers on the tiny graph beside the illustration to make each stitch — bring your needle up from the back of the work on odd numbers and down through the front of the work on even numbers.

Before beginning, read the Stitching Instructions for each section of the project to get an overview of what you'll be doing. You'll find that some pieces are stitched using colors and stitches indicated on graphs, and for other pieces you will be given a color and stitch to use to cover the entire piece.

Cut yarn lengths no longer than 18" to prevent fraying. Thread needle; do not tie a knot in the end. Bring your needle up through the canvas from the back, leaving a short length of yarn on the wrong side of the canvas. As you begin to stitch, work over this short length of yarn. If you are beginning with Continental Stitches, leave a 1" length, but if you are working longer stitches, leave a longer length.

In order for graph colors to contrast well, stitch colors may not match yarn colors. For instance, a light yellow may be selected to represent the metallic cord color gold, or a light blue may represent white yarn.

When following a graph showing several colors, you may want to work all the stitches of one color at the same time. Some stitchers prefer to work with several colors at once by threading each on a separate needle and letting the yarn not being used hang on the wrong side of the work. Either way, remember that strands of yarn which are run across the wrong side of the work may show through the stitches from the front.

As you stitch, try to maintain an even tension on the yarn. Loose stitches will look uneven, and tight stitches will let the canvas show through. If your yarn twists as you work, you may want to let your needle and yarn hang and untwist occasionally.

When you end a section of stitching or finish a thread, weave the yarn through the back side of your last few stitches, then trim it off.

Castle Construction & Assembly

After all pieces of an item are stitched, the order of assembly is listed in the Stitching Instructions and illustrated in diagrams found with the graphs. For best results, join pieces in the order written. Refer to the Stitch Key and to the directives near the graphs for precise attachments. When attaching a straight edge to a curved edge, you may want to tack the pieces together before Whipstitching. Remove tacking after the pieces are joined.

NOTE: The walls of the castle are joined by Whipstitching through several thicknesses. A curved needle must be used to join some walls. If the stitches joining the upper and lower walls are done too tightly, the walls will not stand straight.

Cross Stitch Illustration

Backstitch Illustration

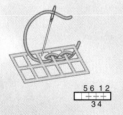

Gluing and Finishing Tips

To combat glue strings when using a hot glue gun, practice a swirling motion as you work. After placing the drop of glue on your work, lift the gun slightly and swirl to break the stream of glue, as if you were making an ice cream cone. Have a cup of water handy when gluing. For those times that you'll need to touch the glue, first dip your finger into the water just enough to dampen it. This will minimize the glue sticking to your finger, and it will cool and set the glue more quickly.

To attach beads, use a bit more glue to form a cup around the bead. If too much shows after drying, use a craft knife to trim off excess glue.

If desired, stiffen ribbons cut for flags with a fabric stiffener before embellishing.

Scotchguard® or other fabric protectors may be used on your finished projects. However, avoid using a permanent marker if you plan to use a fabric protector, and be sure to remove all other markings before stitching. Fabric protectors can cause markings to bleed, staining yarn.

To remove yarn "fuzz"and make your project look new again, shave with a fabric shaver.

For More Information

For supplies, shop your local craft and needlework stores. If you are unable to find the supplies you need, write to the address below for a free catalog. *The Needlecraft Shop* carries a wide variety of plastic canvas supplies, including craft cutters for plastic canvas.

Sometimes even the most experienced needlecrafters can find themselves having trouble following instructions. If you have difficulty completing your project, write to Plastic Canvas Editors, *The Needlecraft Shop*, 23 Old Pecan Road, Big Sandy, Texas 75755.

13

Fashion Doll DREAM CASTLE

SIZE: Castle is 28" x 54" x 32" tall, not including flags.
MATERIALS FOR CASTLE:
NOTE: For combined materials for castle and furnishings, see page 146.

- [ ] 96 sheets of stiff 12" x 18" or larger 7-count plastic canvas
- [ ] Two sheets of standard-size (regular flexibility) 7-count plastic canvas
- [ ] Scraps of white 7-count plastic canvas
- [ ] 1 yd. white 54"-wide felt
- [ ] 45" wooden ⅛" dowel
- [ ] Two 12¾" wooden ½" dowels (optional; paint white)
- [ ] 1⅛ yds. white 7" lace
- [ ] 13 gold 5-mm. beads
- [ ] 32 gold 3-mm. beads
- [ ] 37 silver 4-mm. beads
- [ ] 42 silver 3-mm. beads
- [ ] Five white 15-mm. aurora borealis berry beads
- [ ] 12" of prestrung clear aurora borealis beads
- [ ] 18 blue 5-mm. faceted beads
- [ ] 6¼" heavy gauge floral or clothes hanger wire
- [ ] 16" of white and 2" of tan ¾"-wide Velcro® closures
- [ ] 12" each of 1½"-wide lt. and dk. teal heavy satin ribbon
- [ ] One 2½" x 3½" and one 2½" x 5" piece of craft or aluminum foil
- [ ] Four pictures from magazines or encyclopedias (two 2¾" x 5½" and two 2½" x 3")
- [ ] Silver glitter fabric paint
- [ ] Silver acrylic paint
- [ ] Two 1½"-wide lion's head drawer pulls
- [ ] One two-hole drawer pull backplate with 3" between holes (backplate in photo is 1⅛" x 5½")
- [ ] Two ½"-long No. 8 brass screws with nuts (32 threads per inch)

- [ ] Craft glue or glue gun
- [ ] Sewing needle and white thread
- [ ] Six-strand embroidery floss:
  - [ ] Gray – ½ yd.
- [ ] Metallic cord:
  - [ ] White/Silver – 130 yds.
  - [ ] White/Gold – 97 yds.
- [ ] Worsted-weight or plastic canvas yarn:

NylonPlus™	Needloft™
[ ] #02	#00 Black – 4½ oz.
[ ] #11	#07 Pink – 60 yds.
[ ] #35	#13 Maple – 16½ oz.
[ ] #36	#15 Brown – 4 yds.
[ ] #27	#17 Gold – 3½ oz.
[ ] #33	#18 Tan – 50 yds.
[ ] #42	#21 Baby Yellow – 42 yds.
[ ] #30	#24 Mint – 4 yds.
[ ] #28	#26 Baby Green – 2½ oz.
[ ] #32	#29 Forest – 6 yds.
[ ] #59	#30 Avocado – 11 yds.
[ ] #38	#34 Cerulean – 23 yds.
[ ] #23	#38 Gray – 35 oz.
[ ] #24	#39 Eggshell – 4 oz.
[ ] #01	#41 White – 55 oz.
[ ] #34	#43 Camel – 61 yds.
[ ] #22	#45 Lilac – 2½ oz.
[ ] #21	#46 Purple – 6 yds.
[ ] #46	#47 Peach – 3½ oz.
[ ] #08	#50 Teal Blue – 28 yds.
[ ] #60	#51 Aqua – 3 oz.
[ ] #54	#55 Watermelon – 2 yds.
[ ] #26	#57 Yellow – small amount

Dining Room

Bedroom

ining Room

BASE

CUTTING INSTRUCTIONS:

NOTES: Graphs and diagrams on pages 20-23. Use stiff canvas throughout.

A: For left and right base pieces, cut one each according to graphs.

B-E: For vertical base support pieces, cut number indicated according to graphs.

F-I: For horizontal base support pieces, cut number indicated according to graphs.

J: For back base support, cut one 4 x 113 holes (see graph).

ASSEMBLY INSTRUCTIONS:

NOTE: All pieces are unworked.

1: With White, assemble pieces as indicated on graphs and according to Base Assembly Diagram.

Set aside.

Base Assembly Diagram

Step 2: Working through all thicknesses, Whipstitch one vertical support B along center of overlap area and one along edges of A pieces.

Left A

Back

Right A

Step 1: Overlap 16 holes on each base and baste A pieces together at ends.

Fig. 1

Step 3: Remove basting and Whipstitch remaining vertical supports to base.

Step 4: Whipstitch J to base; tack to vertical supports according to Step 1 of Support Tacking Diagram.

Fig. 2

Support Tacking Diagram

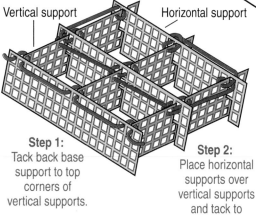

Vertical support

Horizontal support

Step 1: Tack back base support to top corners of vertical supports.

Step 2: Place horizontal supports over vertical supports and tack to secure.

Step 5: Overlapping five holes at one end of G and H pieces as indicated, fit notches together and tack horizontal supports to vertical supports according to Support Interlocking Diagram and Step 2 of Support Tacking Diagram.

Support Interlocking Diagram

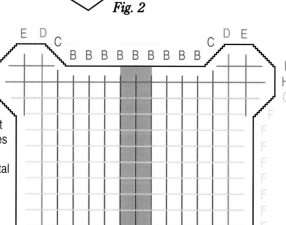

Horizontal support

Vertical supports

Overlap area

Fig. 3

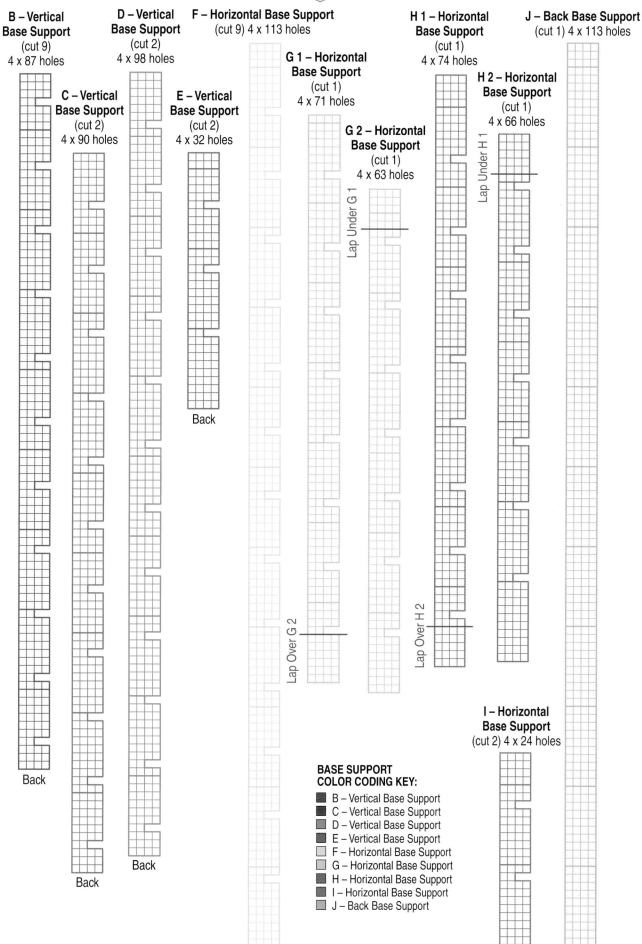

B – Vertical Base Support
(cut 9)
4 x 87 holes

C – Vertical Base Support
(cut 2)
4 x 90 holes

D – Vertical Base Support
(cut 2)
4 x 98 holes

E – Vertical Base Support
(cut 2)
4 x 32 holes

F – Horizontal Base Support
(cut 9) 4 x 113 holes

G 1 – Horizontal Base Support
(cut 1)
4 x 71 holes

G 2 – Horizontal Base Support
(cut 1)
4 x 63 holes

H 1 – Horizontal Base Support
(cut 1)
4 x 74 holes

H 2 – Horizontal Base Support
(cut 1)
4 x 66 holes

I – Horizontal Base Support
(cut 2) 4 x 24 holes

J – Back Base Support
(cut 1) 4 x 113 holes

Lap Under G 1

Lap Over G 2

Lap Under H 1

Lap Over H 2

Back

Back

Back

Back

BASE SUPPORT COLOR CODING KEY:
- B – Vertical Base Support
- C – Vertical Base Support
- D – Vertical Base Support
- E – Vertical Base Support
- F – Horizontal Base Support
- G – Horizontal Base Support
- H – Horizontal Base Support
- I – Horizontal Base Support
- J – Back Base Support

A – Left Base Piece
(cut 1) 80 x 107 holes

WALL ATTACHMENT KEY:
☐ End, Center & Door Wall Attachment
Fireplace & Hutch Interior Attachment

Lap Over

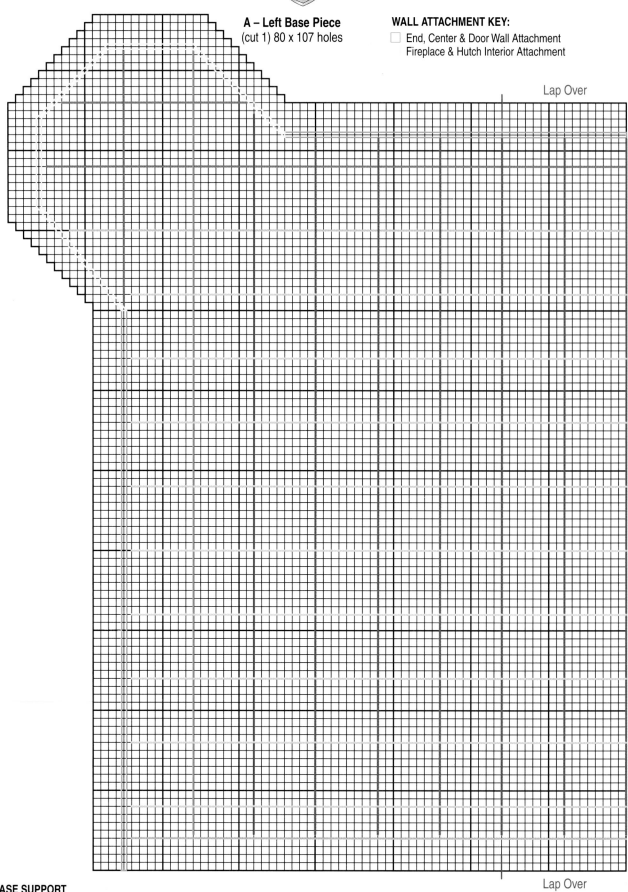

Lap Over

BASE SUPPORT
COLOR CODING KEY:

■ B – Vertical Base Support
■ C – Vertical Base Support
■ D – Vertical Base Support

■ E – Vertical Base Support
☐ F – Horizontal Base Support
☐ G – Horizontal Base Support

■ H – Horizontal Base Support
■ I – Horizontal Base Support
☐ J – Back Base Support

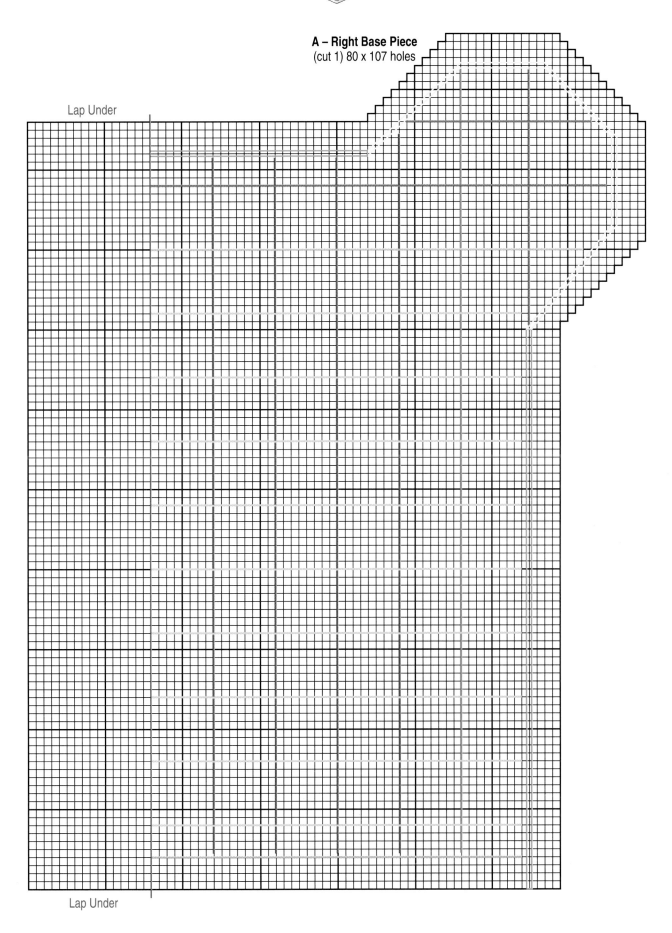

A – Right Base Piece
(cut 1) 80 x 107 holes

Lap Under

Lap Under

FIREPLACE

CUTTING INSTRUCTIONS:

NOTES: Graphs and diagrams on pages 24-26. Use stiff canvas for A-G pieces and clear regular canvas for H.

A: For fireplace interior walls, cut two 16 x 90 holes, two 11 x 90 holes and one 12 x 90 holes (see graphs).

B: For vertical supports, cut three 3 x 90 holes (no graph).

C: For horizontal supports, cut six 3 x 11 holes (no graph).

D: For mantel top, cut one according to graph.

E: For mantel front, cut one according to graph.

F: For lower front, cut one according to graph.

G: For upper front, cut one 29 x 40 holes.

H: For small frame, cut one according to graph.

I: For mirror or painting, using center cutout edges of H as a pattern, cut one from foil or picture ⅛" larger at all edges.

STITCHING INSTRUCTIONS:

NOTE: B and C pieces are unworked.

1: Using colors and stitches indicated, work A, D, E, F and G pieces according to graphs; with White, Overcast F and G as indicated on graphs.

NOTE: Separate floss into 3-ply strands.

2: Using three strands gray floss and Backstitch, embroider candlestick outlines as indicated. With thread, sew eight silver 3-mm. beads to each candlestick according to Candlestick Diagram.

3: With White/Silver, Overcast unfinished inner cutout edges of H.

Holding upper front and frame together as indicated with I between, Whipstitch unfinished outer edge of H to G; working through both thicknesses, work Long Stitch at top of frame according to graph.

4: With White for mantel pieces and with Black, Whipstitch A-E pieces together as indicated and according to Fireplace Assembly Diagram; Overcast unfinished edges of mantel.

Set pieces aside.

DINING ROOM COLOR KEY:

Nylon Plus™ Needloft™ yarn
☐ #02		#00 Black

STITCH KEY:
- ☐ Shelf/Divider Attachment
- ☐ Floor Attachment

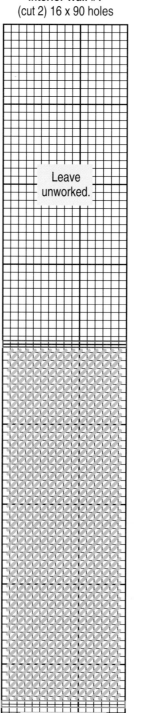

A – Dining Room Fireplace Interior Wall #1
(cut 2) 16 x 90 holes

Leave unworked.

Leave unworked.

A – Dining Room Fireplace Interior Wall #2
(cut 2) 11 x 90 holes

Leave unworked.

Leave unworked.

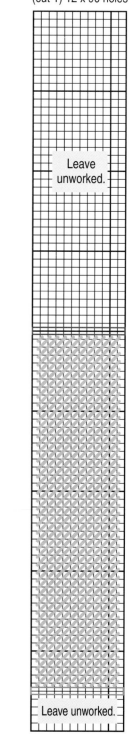

A – Dining Room Fireplace Interior Wall #3
(cut 1) 12 x 90 holes

Leave unworked.

Leave unworked.

Fireplace Assembly Diagram

Step 1:
Whipstitch A#1, A#2 and one
B together.

A#1
(right side)
A#2
(wrong side)

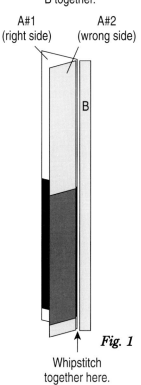

B

Fig. 1

Whipstitch
together here.

Step 2:
Whipstitch remaining
A and B pieces together.

A#1   A#2   A#3   A#2   A#1

B   B   B   B

Fig. 2

Step 3:
Whipstitch B and C
pieces together.

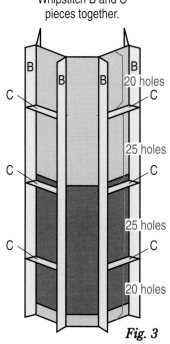

B   B
B   B   B
C   C
20 holes

C   C
25 holes

C   C
25 holes

C   C
20 holes

Fig. 3

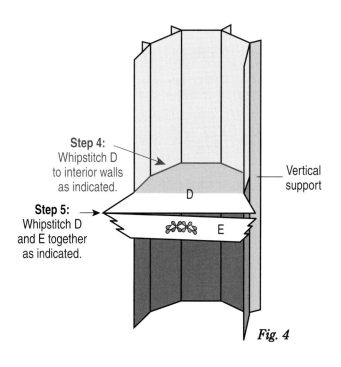

Step 4:
Whipstitch D
to interior walls
as indicated.

Vertical
support

D

Step 5:
Whipstitch D
and E together
as indicated.

E

Fig. 4

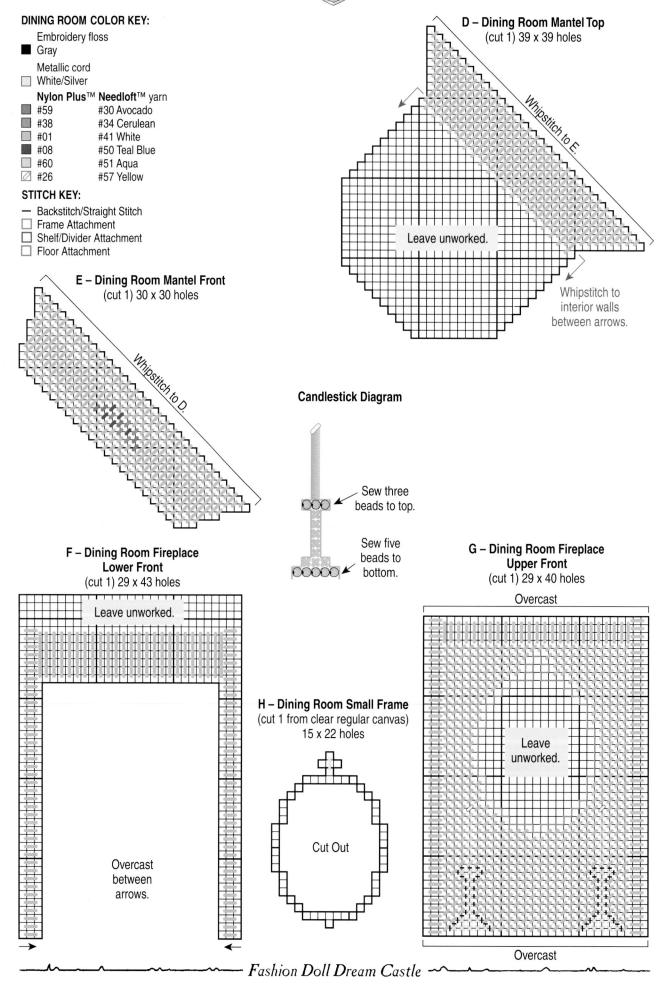

DINING ROOM COLOR KEY:

Embroidery floss
■ Gray

Metallic cord
☐ White/Silver

Nylon Plus™ Needloft™ yarn

■ #59	#30 Avocado
■ #38	#34 Cerulean
■ #01	#41 White
■ #08	#50 Teal Blue
■ #60	#51 Aqua
◨ #26	#57 Yellow

STITCH KEY:

— Backstitch/Straight Stitch
☐ Frame Attachment
☐ Shelf/Divider Attachment
☐ Floor Attachment

D – Dining Room Mantel Top
(cut 1) 39 x 39 holes

Whipstitch to E.

Leave unworked.

Whipstitch to interior walls between arrows.

E – Dining Room Mantel Front
(cut 1) 30 x 30 holes

Whipstitch to D.

Candlestick Diagram

Sew three beads to top.

Sew five beads to bottom.

F – Dining Room Fireplace Lower Front
(cut 1) 29 x 43 holes

Leave unworked.

Overcast between arrows.

H – Dining Room Small Frame
(cut 1 from clear regular canvas)
15 x 22 holes

Cut Out

G – Dining Room Fireplace Upper Front
(cut 1) 29 x 40 holes

Overcast

Leave unworked.

Overcast

HUTCH

CUTTING INSTRUCTIONS:

NOTES: Graphs and diagram on pages 27-28. Use stiff canvas throughout.

A: For interior wall pieces, cut two 16 x 90 holes, two 11 x 90 holes and one 12 x 90 holes (see graphs).

B: For vertical supports, cut four 3 x 90 holes (no graph).

C: For horizontal supports, cut six 3 x 11 holes (no graph).

D: For shelves, cut two according to graph.

E: For front, cut one according to graph.

F: For drawer facade, cut one 7 x 23 holes.

G: For left and right door facades, cut one each 10 x 20 holes.

STITCHING INSTRUCTIONS:

NOTE: B and C pieces are unworked.

1: Using colors and stitches indicated, work A, D and E pieces according to graphs. With White, Overcast unfinished edges of E as indicated on graph and unworked F and G pieces. Holding facades to E as indicated and working through both thicknesses as one, using colors and stitches indicated, work F and G pieces according to facade graphs.

2: With thread, sew one 5-mm. silver bead to each facade as indicated.

3: With White, Whipstitch A-C pieces together according to Steps 1-3 of Fireplace Assembly Diagram on page 25. Whipstitch D pieces to interior walls according to Hutch Assembly Diagram; Overcast unfinished edge of top shelf only.

Set pieces aside.

A – Dining Room Hutch Interior Wall #2
(cut 2) 11 x 90 holes

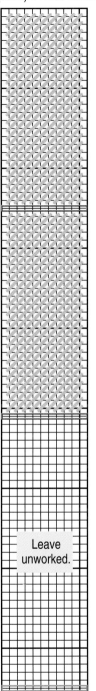

Leave unworked.

A – Dining Room Hutch Interior Wall #3
(cut 1) 12 x 90 holes

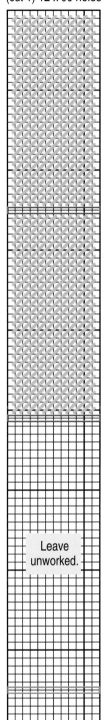

Leave unworked.

A – Dining Room Hutch Interior Wall #1
(cut 2) 16 x 90 holes

Leave unworked.

DINING ROOM COLOR KEY:

Nylon Plus™ Needloft™ yarn

■ #59	#30 Avocado
■ #38	#34 Cerulean
■ #01	#41 White
■ #08	#50 Teal Blue

STITCH KEY:

☐ Shelf/Divider Attachment
☐ Door/Drawer Attachment
○ Bead/Handle Attachment

F – Dining Room Hutch Drawer Facade
(cut 1) 7 x 23 holes

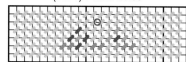

G – Dining Room Hutch Right Door Facade
(cut 1) 10 x 20 holes

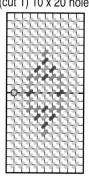

E – Dining Room Hutch Front
(cut 1) 29 x 84 holes
Overcast

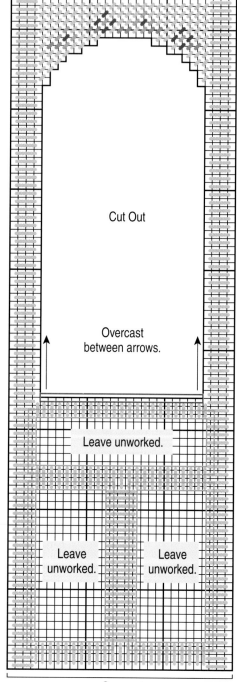

Cut Out

Overcast between arrows.

Leave unworked.

Leave unworked.   Leave unworked.

Overcast

Dining Room Hutch Assembly Diagram

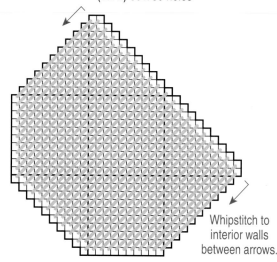

Vertical support

Whipstitch D pieces to interior walls as indicated.

G – Dining Room Hutch Left Door Facade
(cut 1) 10 x 20 holes

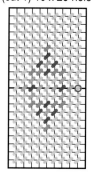

D – Dining Room Hutch Shelf
(cut 2) 30 x 30 holes

Whipstitch to interior walls between arrows.

DINING ROOM INTERIOR

WALL SUPPORT PIECES CUTTING INSTRUCTIONS:

NOTES: Graphs on page 30. Use stiff canvas throughout.

A-H: For vertical wall support pieces, cut number indicated according to graphs.

I-O: For horizontal wall support pieces, cut number indicated according to graphs.

INTERIOR CUTTING INSTRUCTIONS:

NOTES: Graphs, illustrations and diagrams on pages 29 and 31-38. Use stiff canvas for A-E pieces and clear regular canvas for F, H and I.

A: For end wall, cut one according to graph.

B: For center wall, cut one according to graph.

C: For door wall, cut one according to graph.

D: For door arch pieces, cut two 3 x 90 holes (no graph).

E: For left and right floor pieces, cut one each according to graphs.

F: For large frame, cut one according to graph.

G: For mirror or painting, using center cutout edges of F as a pattern, cut one from foil or picture 1/8" larger at all edges.

H: For chandelier, cut one according to graph.

I: For chandelier base, cut one according to graph.

STITCHING INSTRUCTIONS:

NOTE: Wall support pieces and Interior H are unworked.

1: Using colors and stitches indicated, work interior A, B, C and I pieces according to graphs. With White/Silver, Overcast unfinished edges of I and inner cutout edges of F. Holding frame and door wall together as indicated on graph with G between, Whipstitch unfinished outer edge of F to C; working through both thicknesses, work Long Stitch at top of frame according to graph.

2: Overlapping 10 holes at one end and working through both thicknesses at overlap area to join (see Door Arch Overlapping Diagram), using White and Slanted

Door Arch Overlapping Diagram

Gobelin Stitch over narrow width, work D pieces. Whipstitch one edge of arch to wrong side of door wall as indicated.

3: For floor, overlapping 6 holes as indicated and working through both thicknesses at overlap area to join, using colors and stitches indicated, work E pieces.

4: Leaving ends of indicated support pieces unstitched next to windows and doorway, with indicated colors (see Interior Wall Support Attachment Diagram), Whipstitch vertical support pieces to wrong side of walls according to Wall Support Assembly Illustrations.

5: Fit notches together and tack horizontal supports to vertical supports according to Support Interlocking Diagram on page 20 and according to Step 2 of Support Tacking Diagram on page 20.

6: With White, Whipstitch fireplace and hutch interiors and walls to base as indicated on base graphs (see Wall Attachment Key on page 22) and according to Dining Room Interior Assembly Diagram. Place floor inside assembly; with colors to match floor, Whipstitch floor to fireplace, hutch and walls as indicated and to bottom edges of door arch.

7: With White, Whipstitch fireplace pieces and walls together as indicated and according to Fireplace & Wall Assembly Diagram; Whipstitch hutch pieces and walls together according to Hutch & Wall Assembly Diagram. (**NOTE:** Bottom edges of fireplace and hutch fronts are not attached to floor.)

NOTE: Cut nine 1¾" lengths of clear prestrung beads.

8: For chandelier, assemble H and I pieces as indicated and according to Chandelier Assembly & Beading Diagram.

Set pieces aside.

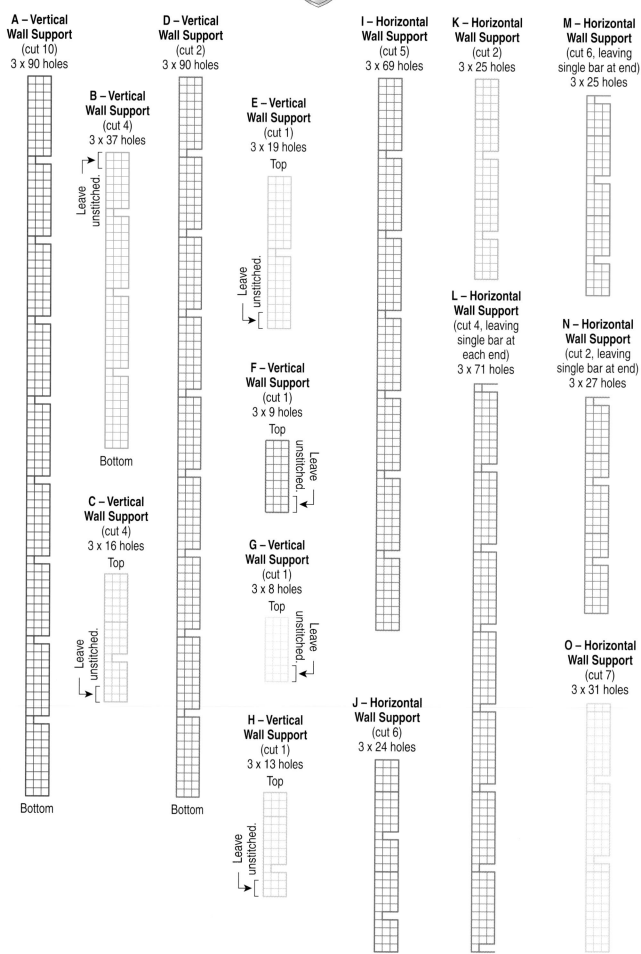

A – Vertical Wall Support
(cut 10)
3 x 90 holes

D – Vertical Wall Support
(cut 2)
3 x 90 holes

I – Horizontal Wall Support
(cut 5)
3 x 69 holes

K – Horizontal Wall Support
(cut 2)
3 x 25 holes

M – Horizontal Wall Support
(cut 6, leaving single bar at end)
3 x 25 holes

B – Vertical Wall Support
(cut 4)
3 x 37 holes

Leave unstitched.

Bottom

E – Vertical Wall Support
(cut 1)
3 x 19 holes

Top

Leave unstitched.

L – Horizontal Wall Support
(cut 4, leaving single bar at each end)
3 x 71 holes

N – Horizontal Wall Support
(cut 2, leaving single bar at end)
3 x 27 holes

C – Vertical Wall Support
(cut 4)
3 x 16 holes

Top

Leave unstitched.

Bottom

F – Vertical Wall Support
(cut 1)
3 x 9 holes

Top

Leave unstitched.

G – Vertical Wall Support
(cut 1)
3 x 8 holes

Top

Leave unstitched.

O – Horizontal Wall Support
(cut 7)
3 x 31 holes

H – Vertical Wall Support
(cut 1)
3 x 13 holes

Top

Leave unstitched.

J – Horizontal Wall Support
(cut 6)
3 x 24 holes

End Wall
Support Assembly Illustration

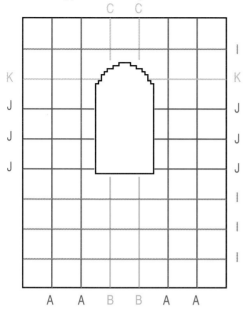

Center Wall
Support Assembly Illustration

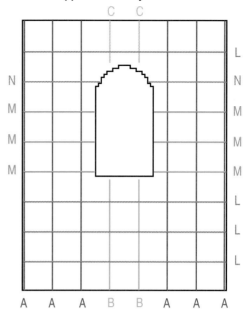

Door Wall
Support Assembly Illustration

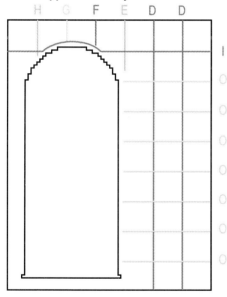

Interior Wall Support Attachment Diagram
(center area not shown)

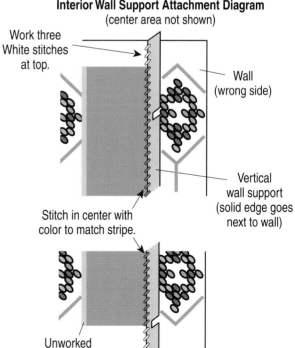

Work three White stitches at top.

Wall (wrong side)

Stitch in center with color to match stripe.

Vertical wall support (solid edge goes next to wall)

Unworked areas

Work ten White stitches at bottom.

WALL SUPPORT COLOR CODING KEY:

- A – Vertical Wall Support
- B – Vertical Wall Support
- C – Vertical Wall Support
- D – Vertical Wall Support
- E – Vertical Wall Support
- F – Vertical Wall Support
- G – Vertical Wall Support
- H – Vertical Wall Support
- I – Horizontal Wall Support
- J – Horizontal Wall Support
- K – Horizontal Wall Support
- L – Horizontal Wall Support
- M – Horizontal Wall Support
- N – Horizontal Wall Support
- O – Horizontal Wall Support

A – Dining Room End Wall
(cut 1) 70 x 90 holes

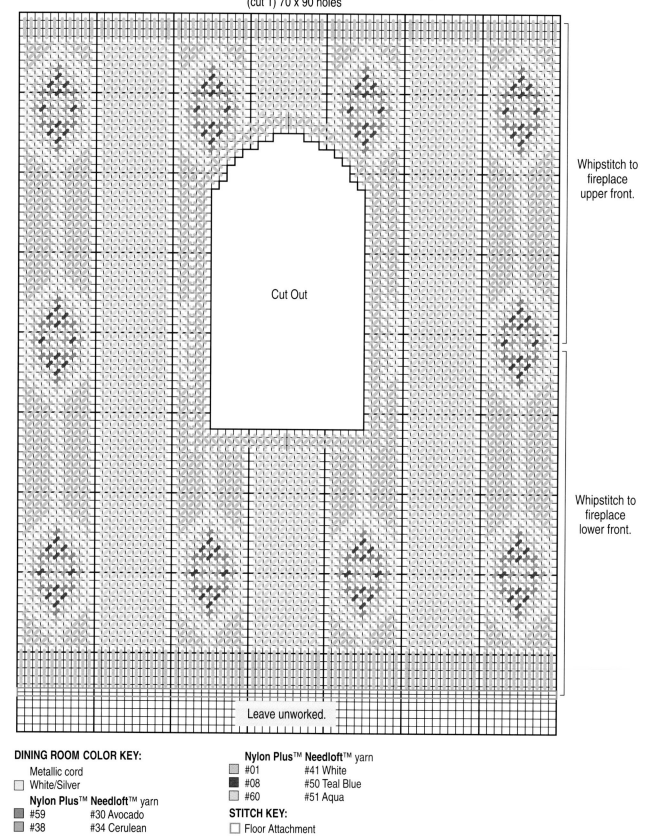

Whipstitch to
fireplace
upper front.

Cut Out

Whipstitch to
fireplace
lower front.

Leave unworked.

DINING ROOM COLOR KEY:

Metallic cord
☐ White/Silver

Nylon Plus™ Needloft™ yarn
■ #59   #30 Avocado
☐ #38   #34 Cerulean

Nylon Plus™ Needloft™ yarn
☐ #01   #41 White
■ #08   #50 Teal Blue
☐ #60   #51 Aqua

STITCH KEY:
☐ Floor Attachment

B – Dining Room Center Wall
(cut 1) 72 x 90 holes

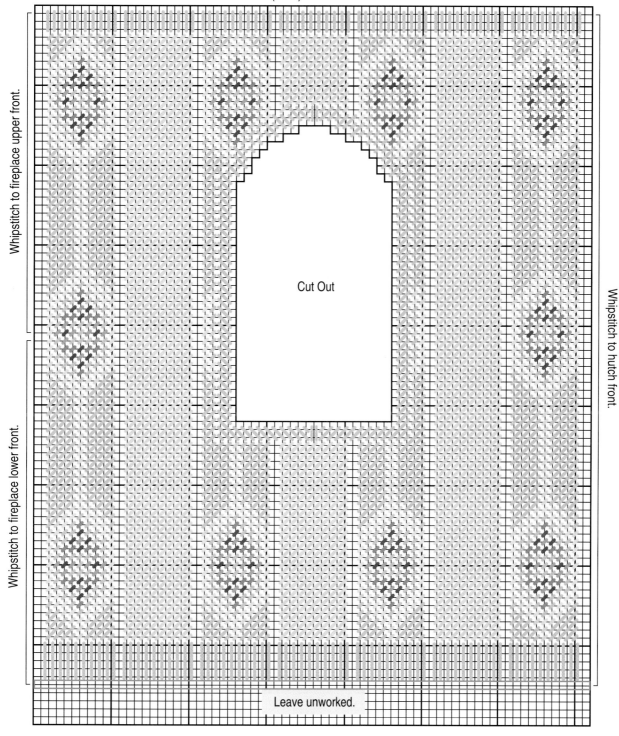

Whipstitch to fireplace upper front.

Whipstitch to fireplace lower front.

Whipstitch to hutch front.

Cut Out

Leave unworked.

C – Dining Room Door Wall
(cut 1) 70 x 90 holes

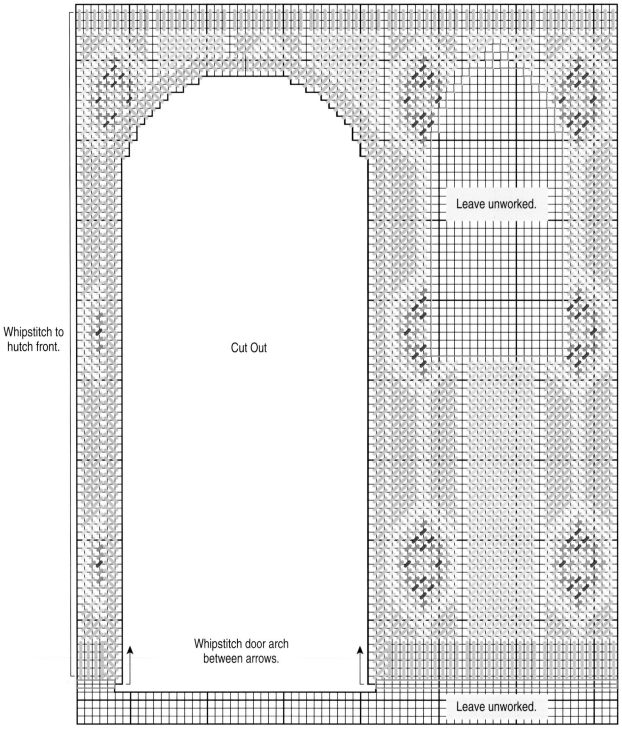

Leave unworked.

Whipstitch to
hutch front.

Cut Out

Whipstitch door arch
between arrows.

Leave unworked.

DINING ROOM COLOR KEY:

Metallic cord
☐ White/Silver

Nylon Plus™ Needloft™ yarn
◼ #59   #30 Avocado
◼ #38   #34 Cerulean
☐ #01   #41 White

Nylon Plus™ Needloft™ yarn
◼ #08   #50 Teal Blue
☐ #60   #51 Aqua

STITCH KEY:
☐ Frame Attachment
☐ Floor Attachment

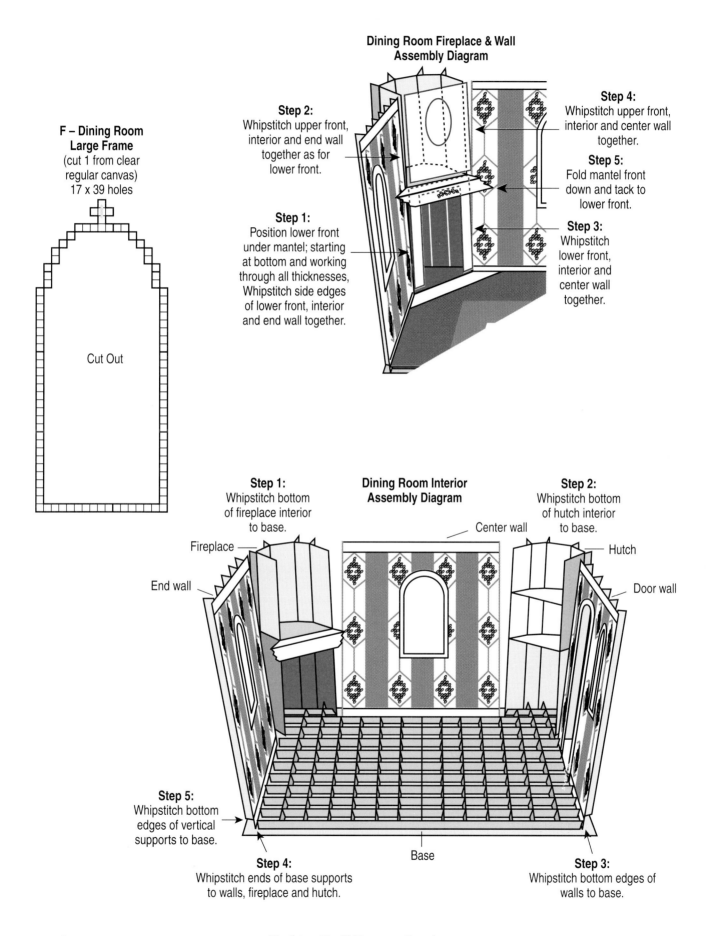

Dining Room Fireplace & Wall Assembly Diagram

F – Dining Room Large Frame
(cut 1 from clear regular canvas)
17 x 39 holes

Cut Out

Step 2:
Whipstitch upper front, interior and end wall together as for lower front.

Step 1:
Position lower front under mantel; starting at bottom and working through all thicknesses, Whipstitch side edges of lower front, interior and end wall together.

Step 4:
Whipstitch upper front, interior and center wall together.

Step 5:
Fold mantel front down and tack to lower front.

Step 3:
Whipstitch lower front, interior and center wall together.

Step 1:
Whipstitch bottom of fireplace interior to base.

Dining Room Interior Assembly Diagram

Step 2:
Whipstitch bottom of hutch interior to base.

Center wall

Fireplace

End wall

Hutch

Door wall

Step 5:
Whipstitch bottom edges of vertical supports to base.

Step 4:
Whipstitch ends of base supports to walls, fireplace and hutch.

Base

Step 3:
Whipstitch bottom edges of walls to base.

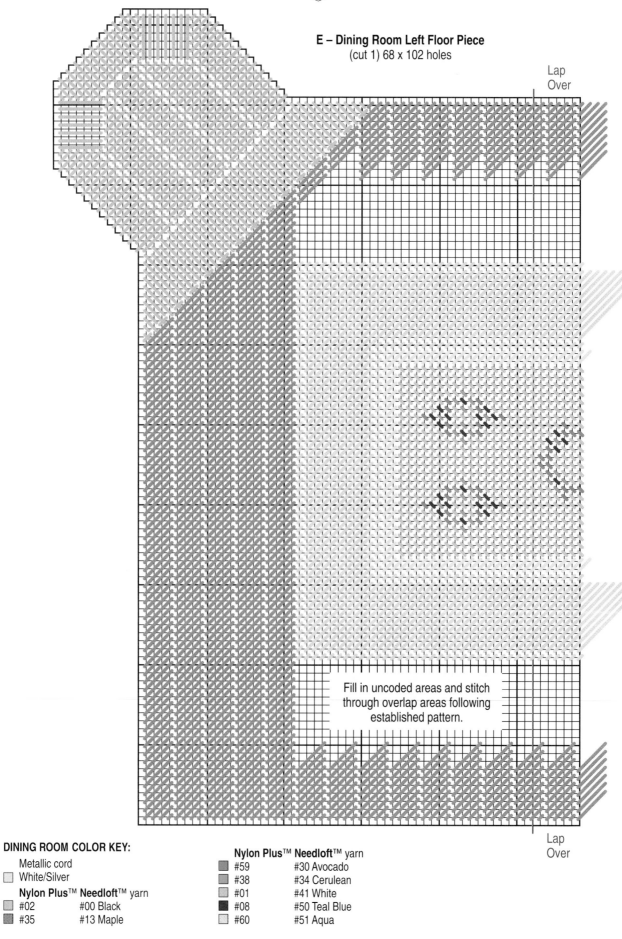

E – Dining Room Left Floor Piece
(cut 1) 68 x 102 holes

Lap
Over

Fill in uncoded areas and stitch
through overlap areas following
established pattern.

Lap
Over

DINING ROOM COLOR KEY:

Metallic cord
☐ White/Silver

Nylon Plus™ **Needloft**™ yarn
☐ #02   #00 Black
☐ #35   #13 Maple

Nylon Plus™ **Needloft**™ yarn
☐ #59
☐ #38
☐ #01
■ #08
☐ #60

#30 Avocado
#34 Cerulean
#41 White
#50 Teal Blue
#51 Aqua

E – Dining Room Right Floor Piece
(cut 1) 73 x 102 holes

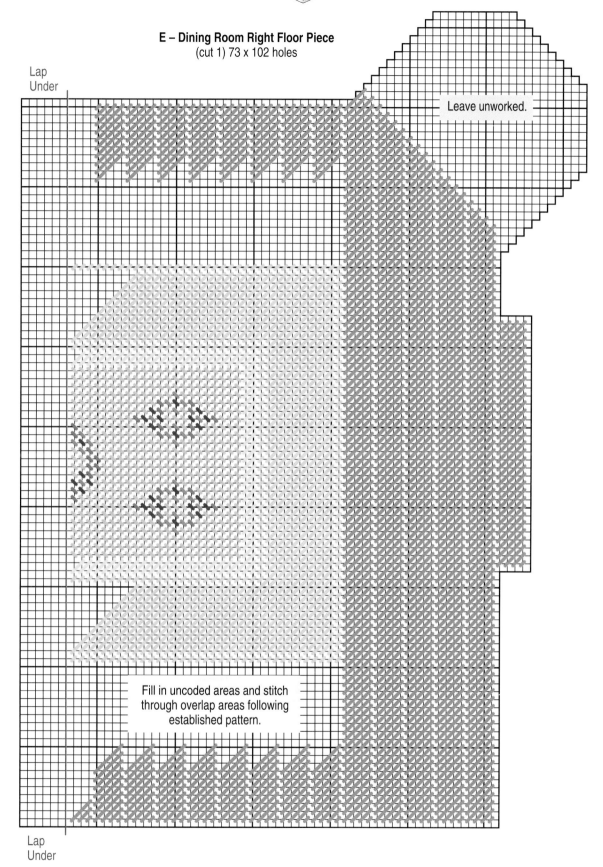

Lap
Under

Leave unworked.

Fill in uncoded areas and stitch
through overlap areas following
established pattern.

Lap
Under

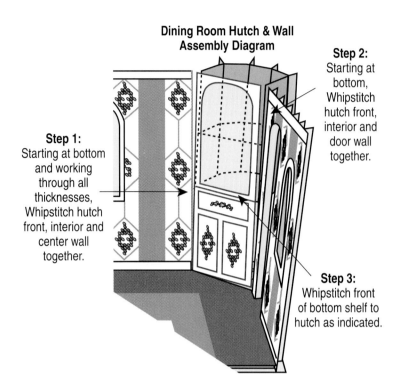

Dining Room Hutch & Wall Assembly Diagram

Step 1:
Starting at bottom and working through all thicknesses, Whipstitch hutch front, interior and center wall together.

Step 2:
Starting at bottom, Whipstitch hutch front, interior and door wall together.

Step 3:
Whipstitch front of bottom shelf to hutch as indicated.

DINING ROOM COLOR KEY:

Metallic cord
☐ White/Silver

I – Chandelier Base
(cut 1 from clear regular canvas)
7 x 7 holes

H – Chandelier
(cut 1 from clear regular canvas) 12 x 39 holes

Sew edges of blue areas together.

Lap Over

Lap Under

Chandelier Assembly & Beading Diagram

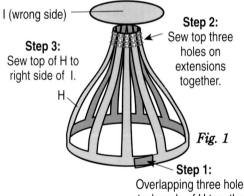

I (wrong side)

Step 3:
Sew top of H to right side of I.

H

Step 2:
Sew top three holes on extensions together.

Fig. 1

Step 1:
Overlapping three holes, tack ends of H together.

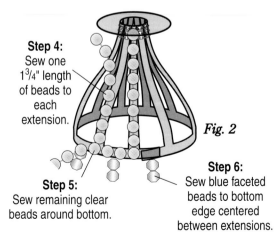

Step 4:
Sew one 1³/₄" length of beads to each extension.

Fig. 2

Step 5:
Sew remaining clear beads around bottom.

Step 6:
Sew blue faceted beads to bottom edge centered between extensions.

LOWER EXTERIOR

CUTTING INSTRUCTIONS:

NOTES: Graphs and diagrams on pages 39-42. Use stiff canvas throughout.

A: For window walls, cut two according to graph.

B: For door wall, cut one according to graph.

C: For turret sides, cut ten 15 x 90 holes.

D: For window frame top pieces, cut two 3 x 84 holes (no graph).

E: For window frame bottom pieces, cut two 3 x 20 holes (no graph).

STITCHING INSTRUCTIONS:

NOTE: B and three C pieces are unworked.

1: Using colors and stitches indicated, work A and seven C pieces according to graphs; with White, Overcast unfinished inner cutout edges of A pieces (leave outer edges unfinished for frame attachment). Using White and Slanted Gobelin Stitch over narrow width, work D and E pieces.

2: With White, Whipstitch one D and one E to wrong side of each A according to Window Frame Assembly Diagram. With indicated colors, Whipstitch A-C pieces together according to Lower Exterior Assembly Diagram.

3: Starting at one end and wrapping pieces around interior according to Lower Exterior Attachment Diagram, Whipstitch bottom edges of exterior to outer edges of base.

4: With White, Whipstitch inner edges of window frames to interior walls and outer edge of door arch to exterior wall. With Maple, Whipstitch floor to exterior door wall at doorway.

Set aside.

Lower Exterior Attachment Diagram

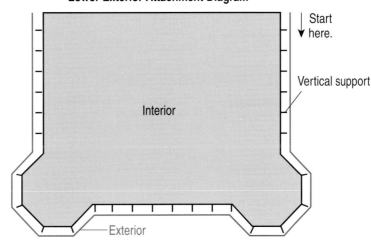

**Dining Room/Bedroom Unit
Lower Exterior Assembly Diagram**

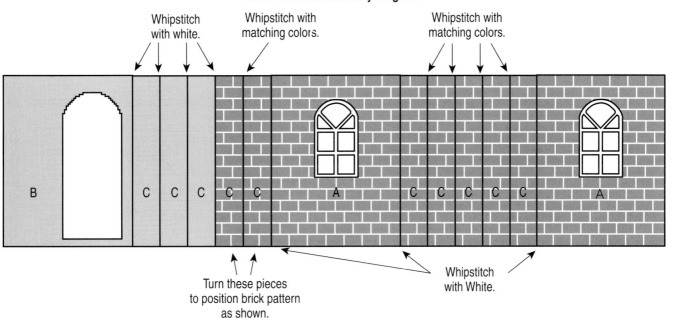

A – Lower Exterior Window Wall
(cut 2) 70 x 90 holes

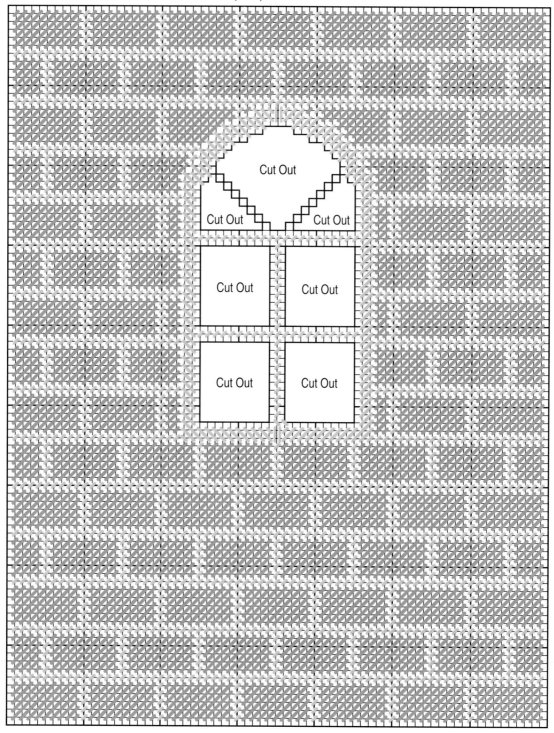

LOWER EXTERIOR COLOR KEY:

Nylon Plus™ Needloft™ yarn

■ #23		#38 Gray
☐ #01		#41 White

C – Lower Exterior Turret Side
(cut 10) 15 x 90 holes

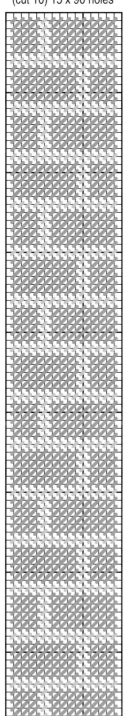

Window Frame Assembly Diagram

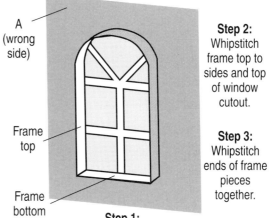

A
(wrong side)

Frame top

Frame bottom

Step 1:
With right side facing up, Whipstitch frame bottom to bottom edge of window cutout.

Step 2:
Whipstitch frame top to sides and top of window cutout.

Step 3:
Whipstitch ends of frame pieces together.

B – Lower Exterior Door Wall
(cut 1) 70 x 90 holes

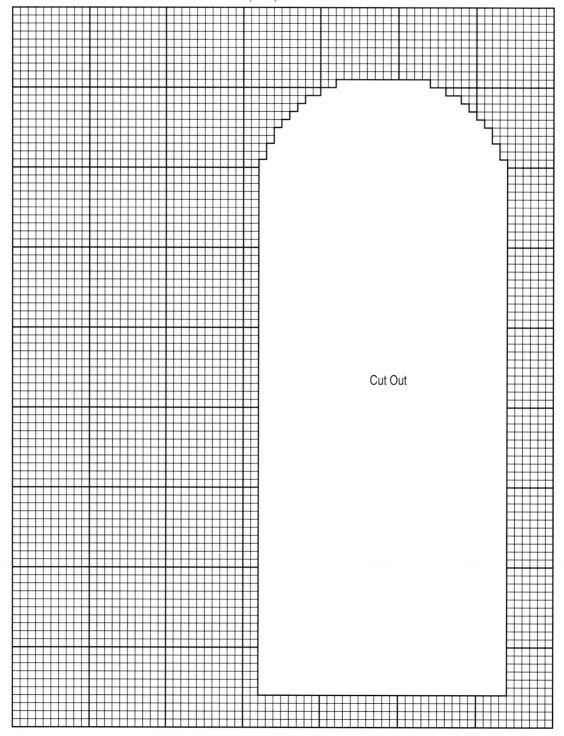

Cut Out

Bedroom

BASE

CUTTING & ASSEMBLY INSTRUCTIONS:

Follow Cutting and Assembly Instructions for Dining Room Base on page 20.

For lower floor ceiling, after base is completed, using bottom of base as a pattern, cut one from felt ⅛" smaller at all edges. Glue felt to bottom of base, leaving outer ¾" unattached.

Set aside.

FIREPLACE

CUTTING INSTRUCTIONS:

Using Bedroom Mantel Front graph on page 44 for E piece, follow Dining Room Fireplace Cutting Instructions on page 24.

STITCHING INSTRUCTIONS:

Substituting Lilac for Aqua on G piece, follow Stitching Instructions for Dining Room Fireplace on page 24.

Set pieces aside.

CLOSET

CUTTING INSTRUCTIONS:

NOTES: Graphs and diagrams on pages 43-45. Use stiff canvas throughout.

A: For interior walls, cut two 16 x 90 holes, two 11 x 90 holes and one 12 x 90 holes (see graphs).

B: For vertical supports, cut four 3 x 90 holes (no graph).

C: For horizontal supports, cut six 3 x 11 holes (no graph).

D: For dividers, cut three according to Dining Room Hutch D graph on page 28.

E: For front, cut one according to graph.

F: For door front, cut one according to graph.

G: For door back, cut one 19 x 40 holes (no graph).

H: For mirror, using G as a pattern, cut one from foil ⅛" smaller at all edges.

I: For drawer fronts, cut two 10 x 23 holes.

J: For inner drawer sides, cut four 7 x 17 holes and four 7 x 19 holes (no graphs).

K: For drawer bottoms, cut two 17 x 19 holes (no graph).

L: For handles, cut three according to graph.

M: For closet latch, cut one 4 x 9 holes (no graph).

STITCHING INSTRUCTIONS:

NOTE: A-D, G, J, and K pieces are unworked.

1: Using colors and stitches indicated, work E (hold M to wrong side as indicated and work through both thicknesses to attach latch), F and I pieces according to graphs. (**NOTE:** Remainder of latch is unworked.) With White, Overcast unfinished top and bottom edges of E and outside edges of F pieces as indicated and unfinished edges of I pieces.

2: With White/Silver, Overcast unfinished cutout edges of F; assemble F, G and H pieces according to Door Assembly Diagram. Attach one L to each drawer and door front according to Handle Attachment Diagram. With White, Whipstitch door to closet front as indicated.

3: With White, Whipstitch A-C pieces together according to Steps 1-3 of Fireplace Assembly Diagram on page 25. Whipstitch D pieces together and attach 6¼" wire according to Bedroom Closet Assembly Diagram.

4: With White, assemble each drawer according to Drawer Assembly Diagram.

Set pieces aside.

Bedroom Closet Assembly Diagram

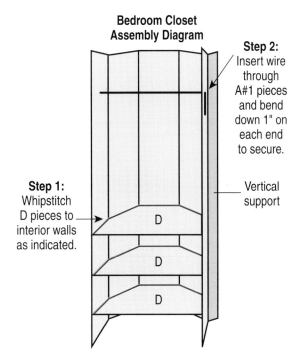

Step 2: Insert wire through A#1 pieces and bend down 1" on each end to secure.

Vertical support

Step 1: Whipstitch D pieces to interior walls as indicated.

BEDROOM COLOR KEY:

Metallic cord
☐ White/Silver

Nylon Plus™ Needloft™ yarn
☐ #01   #41 White

STITCH KEY:
☐ Shelf/Divider Attachment
☐ Door/Drawer Attachment
○ Bead/Handle Attachment
☐ Floor Attachment
☐ Closet Latch Attachment
☐ Closet Door Back Attachment
★ Wire Placement

**A – Bedroom Closet
Interior Wall #1**
(cut 2) 16 x 90 holes

**A – Bedroom Closet
Interior Wall #2**
(cut 2) 11 x 90 holes

**A – Bedroom Closet
Interior Wall #3**
(cut 1) 12 x 90 holes

E – Bedroom Mantel Front
(cut 1) 30 x 30 holes

Whipstitch to D.

E – Bedroom Closet Front
(cut 1) 29 x 84 holes

Overcast

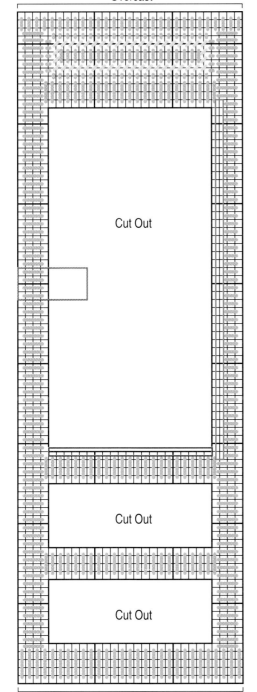

Cut Out

Cut Out

Cut Out

Overcast

F – Bedroom Closet Door Front
(cut 1) 23 x 45 holes

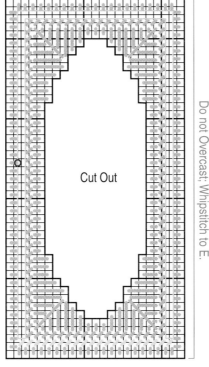

Cut Out

Do not Overcast; Whipstitch to E.

I – Bedroom Closet Drawer Front
(cut 2) 10 x 23 holes

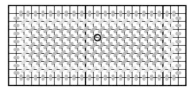

L – Bedroom Closet Handle
(cut 3) 2 x 2 holes
Cut around black bars.

Door Assembly Diagram

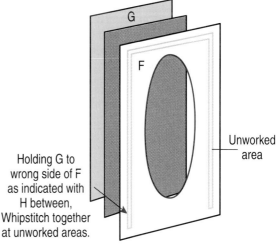

G

F

Unworked area

Holding G to wrong side of F as indicated with H between, Whipstitch together at unworked areas.

Closet Handle Diagram

Insert yarn from back to front through door or drawer as indicated; starting at one corner, wrap entire handle until completely covered; then run yarn back through beginning hole and secure on wrong side.

L

Drawer Assembly Diagram

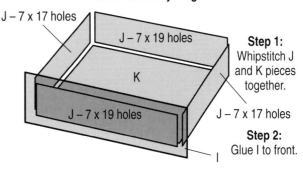

J – 7 x 17 holes
J – 7 x 19 holes
K
J – 7 x 19 holes
J – 7 x 17 holes
I

Step 1: Whipstitch J and K pieces together.

Step 2: Glue I to front.

BEDROOM INTERIOR

WALL SUPPORT PIECES CUTTING INSTRUCTIONS:

Follow Dining Room Interior Wall Support Pieces Cutting Instructions on page 29.

INTERIOR CUTTING INSTRUCTIONS:

A-G: Follow Steps A-G of Dining Room Interior Cutting Instructions on page 29.

STITCHING INSTRUCTIONS:

NOTE: Wall support pieces are unworked.

1: Substituting Lilac for Aqua and working Bedroom Wall Motif (see Rosebud Stitch Illustration) in place of Dining Room Motif, work interior A-C pieces according to graphs.

2: With White/Silver, Overcast inner cutout edges of F. Holding frame and door wall together as indicated on graph with G between, Whipstitch unfinished outer edge of F to C; working through both thicknesses, work Long Stitch at top of frame according to graph.

3: Omitting rug from floor, follow Steps 2-5 of Dining Room Interior Stitching Instructions on page 29.

4: Substituting Bedroom Closet for Dining Room Hutch, follow Steps 6 and 7 of Dining Room Interior Stitching Instructions. Sew or glue 1" piece of white closure to closet latch and corresponding area on door. Slide drawers into closet cutouts.

Set aside.

BEDROOM COLOR KEY:

Metallic cord
☐ White/Silver

Nylon Plus™ Needloft™ yarn

▨	#32		#29 Forest
▪	#23		#38 Gray
☐	#01		#41 White
☐	#22		#45 Lilac
▪	#21		#46 Purple

Bedroom Wall Motif

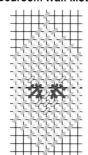

Rosebud Stitch Illustration

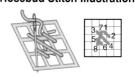

UPPER EXTERIOR

CUTTING INSTRUCTIONS:

NOTES: Graphs and diagrams on pages 46-50. Use stiff canvas for A-D pieces and clear regular canvas for E and F pieces.

A: For window walls, cut two according to graph.

B: For door wall, cut one according to graph.

C: For corner turret sides, cut five according to graph.

D: For center turret sides, cut three #1 pieces and one each of #2 and #3 pieces according to graphs.

E: For window frame tops, cut two 3 x 84 holes (no graph).

F: For window frame bottoms, cut two 3 x 20 holes (no graph).

STITCHING INSTRUCTIONS:

NOTE: B piece is unworked.

1: Using colors and stitches indicated, work A, C and D pieces according to graphs; with White, Overcast unfinished inner cutout edges of A pieces (leave outer edges unfinished for frame attachment). Using White and Slanted Gobelin Stitch over narrow width, work E and F pieces.

2: With White, Whipstitch one E and F piece to wrong side of each A according to Window Frame Assembly Diagram on page 41.

3: Place Bedroom Interior assembly on top of Dining Room; working through all thicknesses and using curved needle, with White, Whipstitch upper and lower walls together according to Upper & Lower Room Assembly Diagram. (**NOTE:** Top edges of fireplace and hutch are not attached to base.)

4: With indicated colors, assemble pieces according to Upper Exterior Assembly Diagram.

5: With White, Whipstitch inner edges of window frames to interior walls and outer edge of door arch to exterior wall. With Maple, Whipstitch floor to exterior door wall at doorway.

Set aside.

Upper & Lower Room Assembly Diagram

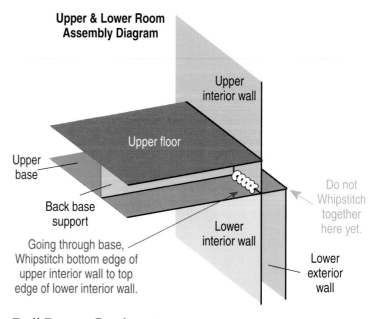

Upper interior wall

Upper floor

Upper base

Back base support

Going through base, Whipstitch bottom edge of upper interior wall to top edge of lower interior wall.

Lower interior wall

Do not Whipstitch together here yet.

Lower exterior wall

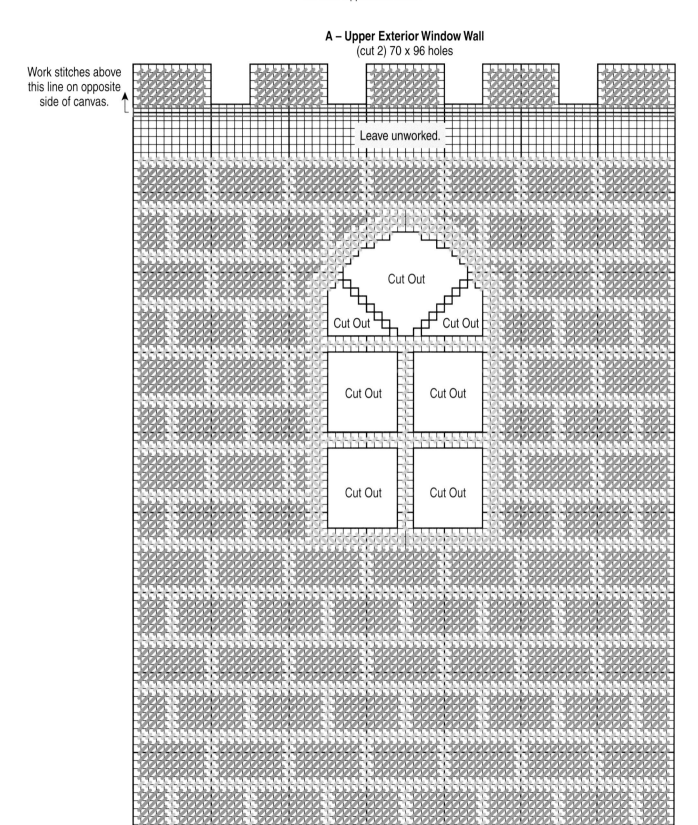

STITCH KEY:
☐ Wall Topper Attachment

A – Upper Exterior Window Wall
(cut 2) 70 x 96 holes

Work stitches above this line on opposite side of canvas.

Leave unworked.

Cut Out

Cut Out   Cut Out

Cut Out   Cut Out

Cut Out   Cut Out

B – Upper Exterior Door Wall
(cut 1) 70 x 90 holes

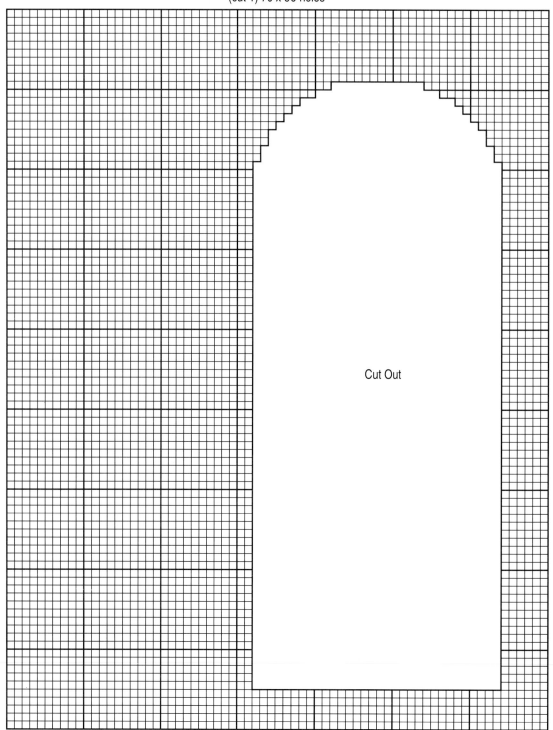

Cut Out

UPPER EXTERIOR COLOR KEY:

Nylon Plus™ **Needloft**™ yarn
#23   #38 Gray
#01   #41 White

C – Corner Turret Side
(cut 5) 15 x 108 holes

D – Center Turret Side #1
(cut 3) 15 x 120 holes

D – Center Turret Side #2
(cut 1) 15 x 120 holes

D – Center Turret Side #3
(cut 1) 15 x 120 holes

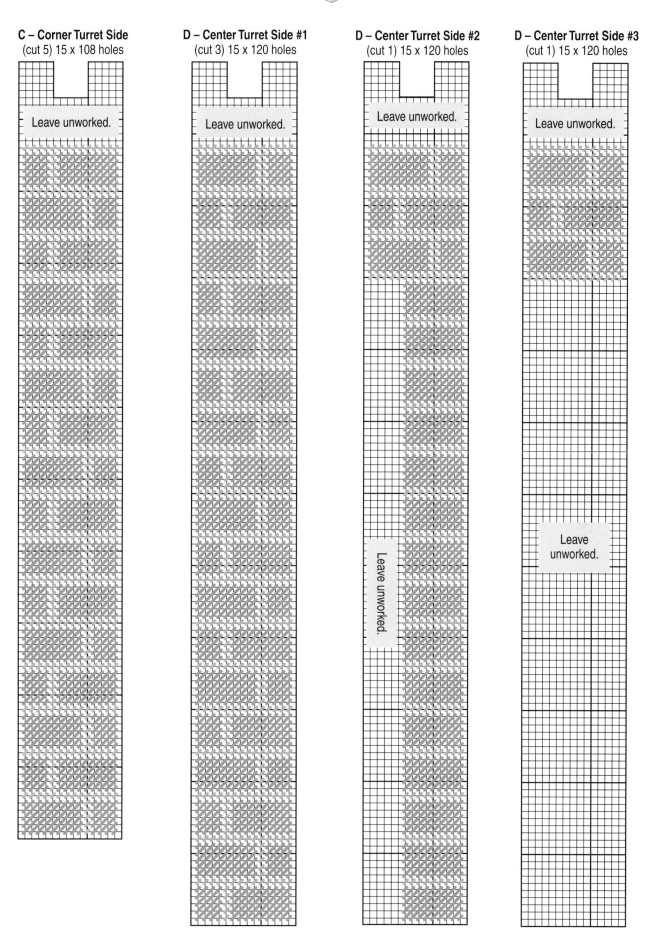

Upper Exterior Assembly Diagram

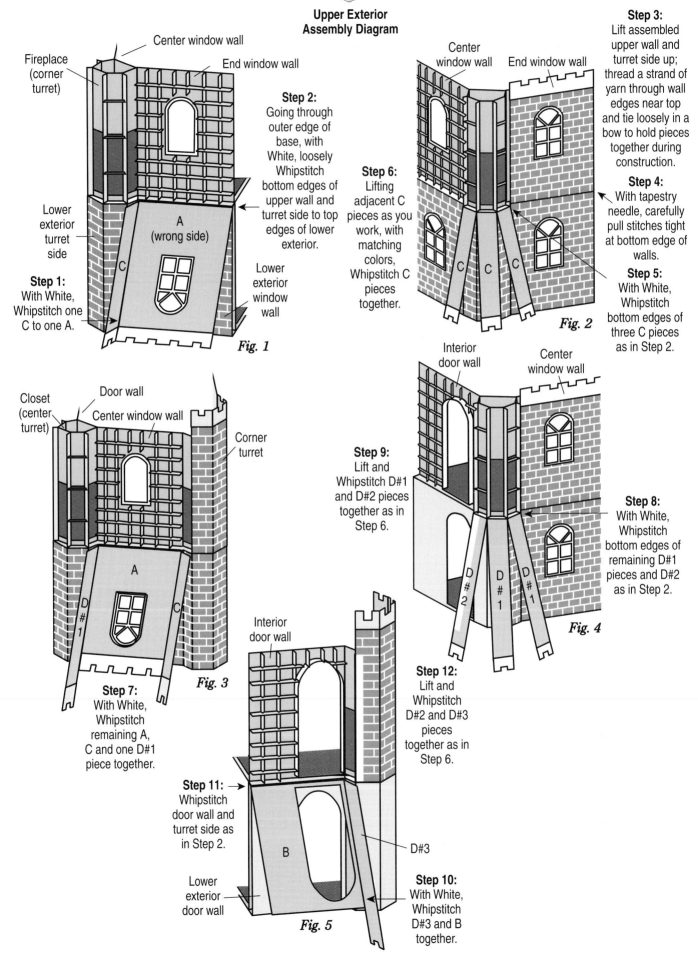

Fireplace (corner turret)

Center window wall

End window wall

Step 2:
Going through outer edge of base, with White, loosely Whipstitch bottom edges of upper wall and turret side to top edges of lower exterior.

Lower exterior turret side

A (wrong side)

C

Step 1:
With White, Whipstitch one C to one A.

Lower exterior window wall

Step 6:
Lifting adjacent C pieces as you work, with matching colors, Whipstitch C pieces together.

Fig. 1

Center window wall

End window wall

Step 3:
Lift assembled upper wall and turret side up; thread a strand of yarn through wall edges near top and tie loosely in a bow to hold pieces together during construction.

Step 4:
With tapestry needle, carefully pull stitches tight at bottom edge of walls.

Step 5:
With White, Whipstitch bottom edges of three C pieces as in Step 2.

C   C   C

Fig. 2

Closet (center turret)

Door wall

Center window wall

Corner turret

A

C

D #1

Step 7:
With White, Whipstitch remaining A, C and one D#1 piece together.

Fig. 3

Interior door wall

Center window wall

Step 9:
Lift and Whipstitch D#1 and D#2 pieces together as in Step 6.

Step 8:
With White, Whipstitch bottom edges of remaining D#1 pieces and D#2 as in Step 2.

D #2   D #1   D #1

Fig. 4

Interior door wall

Step 12:
Lift and Whipstitch D#2 and D#3 pieces together as in Step 6.

Step 11:
Whipstitch door wall and turret side as in Step 2.

B

D#3

Lower exterior door wall

Step 10:
With White, Whipstitch D#3 and B together.

Fig. 5

FINISHING

NOTE: Flags and curtains may be assembled after all three sections of the castle are completed.

CUTTING INSTRUCTIONS:

NOTES: Graphs, illustration and diagrams on pages 51-55. Use stiff canvas throughout.

A: For turret top pieces, cut two according to graph.

B: For wall topper pieces, cut three 4 x 70 holes.

C: For wall trim pieces, cut two according to graph.

D: For turret outer trim pieces, cut ten according to graph.

E: For corner turret inner trim pieces, cut one of #1, three of #2 and one of #3 according to graphs.

F: For center turret inner trim pieces, cut one of #1, three of #2 and one of #3 according to graphs.

G: For turret trim mortar pieces, cut eight 1 x 12 holes, four 1 x 17 holes and four 1 x 29 holes (no graphs).

H: For interior and exterior wall end pieces, cut two each 4 x 90 holes.

I: For wall end support pieces, cut two 4 x 11 holes (no graphs).

J: For floor end pieces, cut two 5 x 113 holes (no graph).

K: For floor end support pieces, cut sixteen 4 x 113 holes (no graph).

L: For flagpole bases, cut two according to graph.

M: For flags, cut one each from lt. and dk. teal ribbon according to Flag Pattern.

N: For flagpoles, cut one 10" and one 12½" length of dowel; paint each dowel with acrylic paint.

O: For washers, cut two 5 x 5 holes (no graph).

STITCHING INSTRUCTIONS:

NOTES: G, I and K pieces are unworked.

1: Using colors and stitches indicated, work A-F, H and L pieces according to graphs. Using Maple and Slanted Gobelin Stitch over narrow width, work J pieces. With White, Overcast A pieces as indicated on graph. Using White/Silver and Straight Stitch, embroider detail on C and D pieces as indicated; Overcast unfinished edges of C pieces as indicated and L pieces.

2: With White, assemble A and B pieces as indicated and according to Turret Top & Wall Topper Assembly Illustration. Placing assembled pieces over top of upper floor walls and turrets, Whipstitch toppers to walls as indicated and according to Inside & Outside Wall Topper Assembly Diagrams. Glue inner edges of turret tops to fireplace and closet fronts. (**NOTE:** Backs of turret tops are not attached, making turrets accessible for storage.)

3: Matching top edges, with White/Silver, Whipstitch C pieces to end and center window walls (see Figs. 2 and 4 of Upper Exterior Assembly Diagram on page 50). Glue bottom edge of trim pieces to walls.

4: For each turret outer trim section, with matching colors, Whipstitch five D pieces and four 1 x 12-hole G pieces together according to Turret Outer Trim Assembly Diagram; with White/Silver, Overcast unfinished bottom edges of assembled trim.

5: For corner turret inner trim, assemble E pieces and 1 x 17-hole G pieces according to Corner Turret Inner Trim Assembly Diagram.

6: For center turret inner trim, assemble F pieces and 1 x 29-hole G pieces according to Center Turret

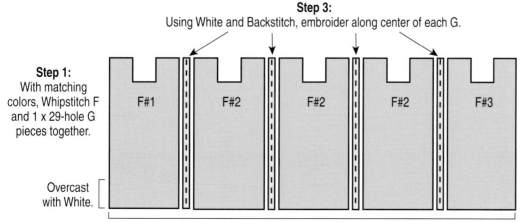

Corner Turret Inner Trim Assembly Diagram

Step 3:
Using White and Backstitch, embroider along center of each G.

Step 1:
With matching colors, Whipstitch E and 1 x 17 hole G pieces together.

Overcast with White.

E#1 · E#2 · E#2 · E#2 · E#3

Step 2:
Overcast side and bottom edges as indicated (see E#1 and E#3 graphs).

Overcast with White.

Overcast with Gray.

Center Turret Inner Trim Assembly Diagram

Step 3:
Using White and Backstitch, embroider along center of each G.

Step 1:
With matching colors, Whipstitch F and 1 x 29-hole G pieces together.

Overcast with White.

F#1 · F#2 · F#2 · F#2 · F#3

Step 2:
Overcast side and bottom edges as indicated (see F#1 graph).

Overcast with Gray.

Inner Trim Assembly Diagram.

7: With White/Silver, assemble corner turret trim according to Corner Turret Finishing Diagram.

8: Assemble center turret trim according to Center Turret Finishing Diagram.

9: To finish each floor, with Maple, assemble one J and eight K pieces according to Floor End Assembly Diagram.

10: Holding H and I pieces together according to Wall Ends Assembly Diagram, with indicated colors, Whipstitch together. To finish walls, with Maple for interior edges of floor ends and with White, Whipstitch wall ends to walls.

11: Glue chandelier base to center of ceiling in lower room.

12: Attaching 12½" flag to center turret, assemble pieces according to Flag Assembly Diagram.

NOTE: Cut four 5"-long pieces of 7" lace.

13: For curtains, glue curved edge of lace pieces to interior walls along top edge of each window.

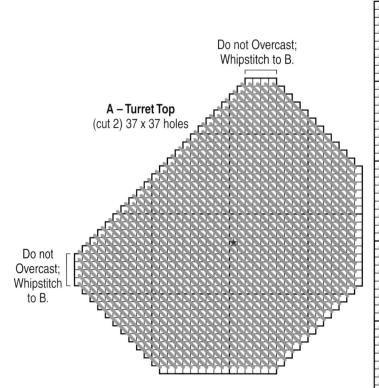

B – Wall Topper
(cut 3) 4 x 70 holes

Do not Overcast;
Whipstitch to B.

A – Turret Top
(cut 2) 37 x 37 holes

Do not
Overcast;
Whipstitch
to B.

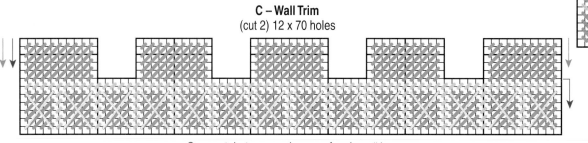

C – Wall Trim
(cut 2) 12 x 70 holes

Overcast between red arrows for piece #1.
Overcast between green arrows for piece #2.

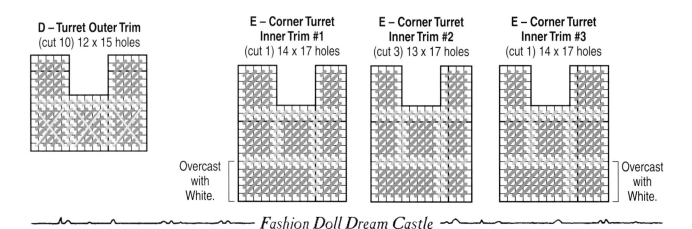

D – Turret Outer Trim
(cut 10) 12 x 15 holes

**E – Corner Turret
Inner Trim #1**
(cut 1) 14 x 17 holes

**E – Corner Turret
Inner Trim #2**
(cut 3) 13 x 17 holes

**E – Corner Turret
Inner Trim #3**
(cut 1) 14 x 17 holes

Overcast
with
White.

Overcast
with
White.

FINISHING COLOR KEY:

Metallic cord
☐ White/Silver

Nylon Plus™ Needloft™ yarn
■ #35   #13 Maple
■ #23   #38 Gray
☐ #01   #41 White

STITCH KEY:

★ Flagpole Placement

M – Flag Pattern
(actual size)

H – Interior Wall End
(cut 2) 4 x 90 holes

H – Exterior Wall End
(cut 2) 4 x 90 holes

L – Flagpole Base
(cut 2) 7 x 7 holes

**F – Center Turret
Inner Trim #1**
(cut 1) 14 x 29 holes

**F – Center Turret
Inner Trim #2**
(cut 3) 13 x 29 holes

**F – Center Turret
Inner Trim #3**
(cut 1) 14 x 29 holes

Overcast
with
White.

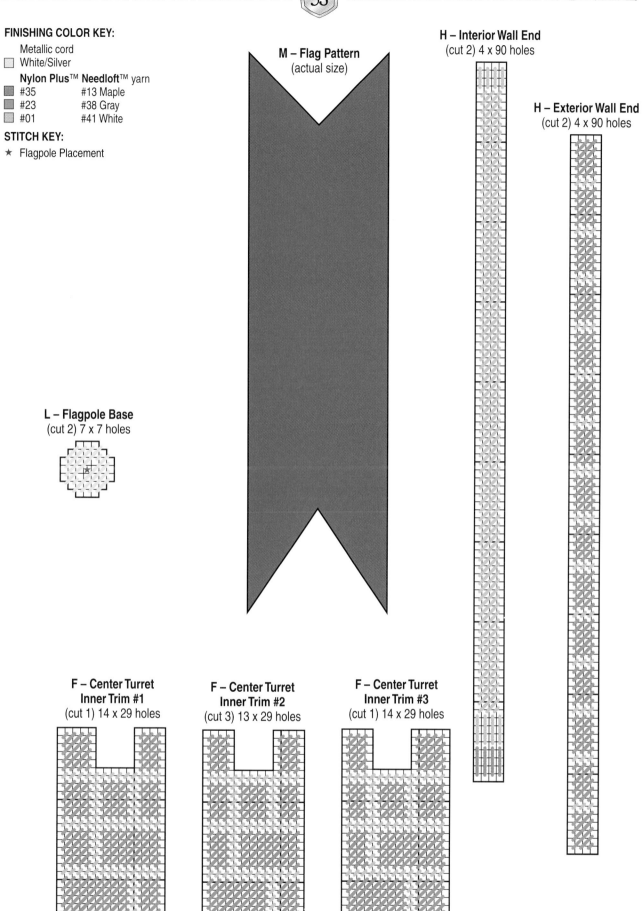

Wall Ends Assembly Diagram

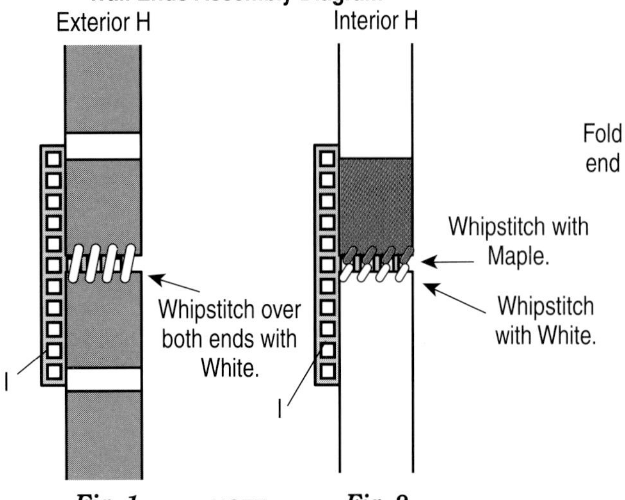

Exterior H

Interior H

Whipstitch over both ends with White.

Whipstitch with Maple.

Whipstitch with White.

I

I

Fig. 1

NOTE:
Supports are shown to one side. When stitching, position directly behind wall ends.

Fig. 2

Flag Assembly Diagram

Step 3:
Glue 5-mm. silver bead to top of dowel.

Step 1:
Fold M in half over end of N and glue together.

Step 2:
With silver glitter paint, outline top and bottom edges of flag.

M

N

Step 4:
Insert bottom of dowel through center of L, then through turret top as indicated on graph.

L

A

O

Step 5:
Slide two O pieces onto bottom of dowel and up against wrong side of turret top; glue to secure.

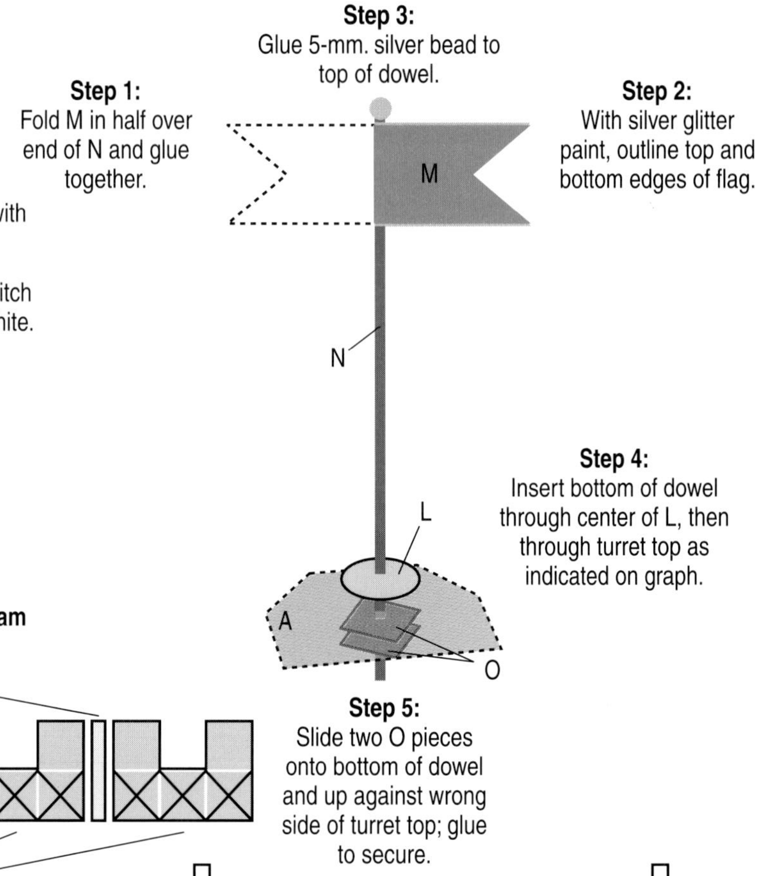

Turret Outer Trim Assembly Diagram

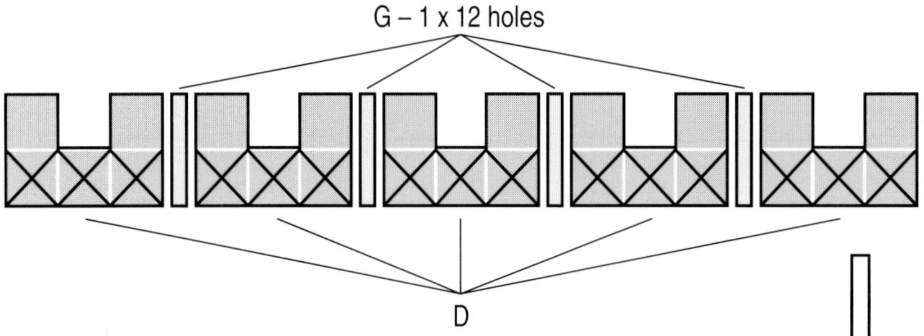

G – 1 x 12 holes

D

Turret Top & Wall Topper Assembly Illustration

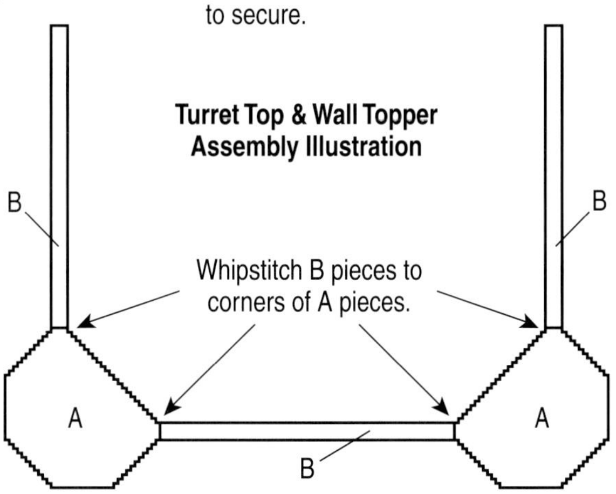

B

B

Whipstitch B pieces to corners of A pieces.

A

A

B

Outside Wall Topper Assembly Diagram

Step 1:
Whipstitch wall toppers to exterior window walls as indicated.

Wall topper

Step 2:
Whipstitch wall toppers to interior window walls.

Interior window wall

Window

Exterior window wall (wrong side)

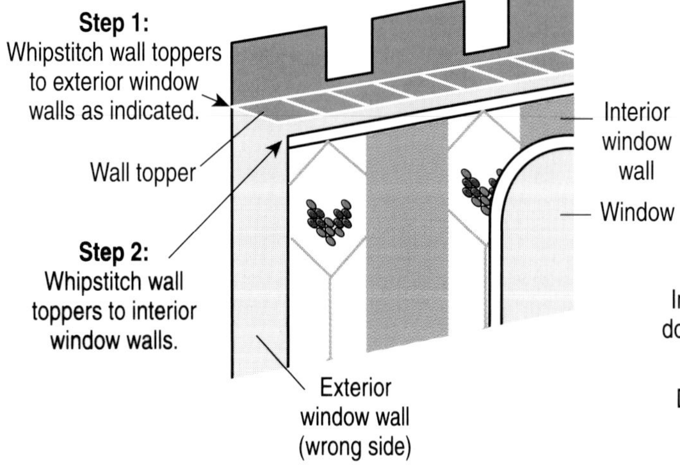

Inside Wall Topper Assembly Diagram

Wall topper

Interior door wall

Doorway

Whipstitch wall topper to door walls.

Exterior door wall (wrong side)

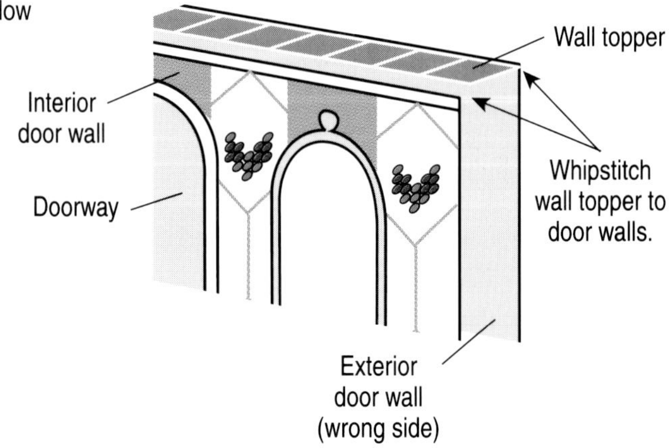

Floor End Assembly Diagram

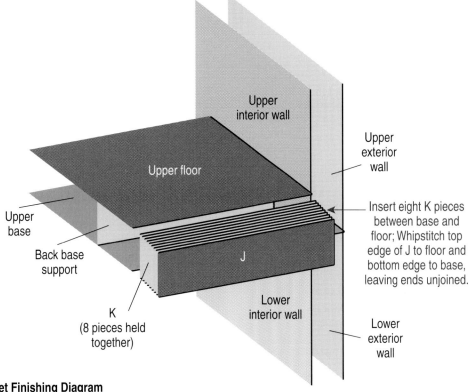

Upper interior wall

Upper floor

Upper exterior wall

Upper base

Back base support

J

K
(8 pieces held together)

Insert eight K pieces between base and floor; Whipstitch top edge of J to floor and bottom edge to base, leaving ends unjoined.

Lower interior wall

Lower exterior wall

Corner Turret Finishing Diagram
(Pieces are shown in different colors for contrast.)

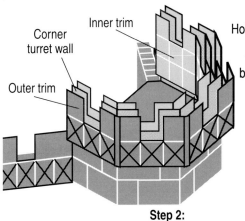

Inner trim

Corner turret wall

Outer trim

Step 1:
Holding inner and outer trim wrong sides together with wall between, Whipstitch unfinished edges together.

Step 2:
Glue bottom edge of exterior trim to walls.

Center Turret Finishing Diagram
(Pieces are shown in different colors for contrast.)

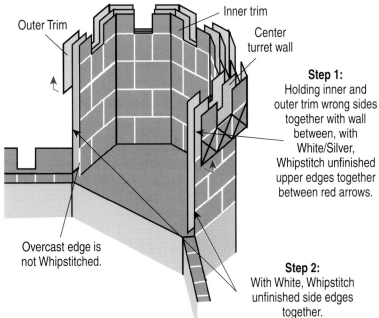

Outer Trim

Inner trim

Center turret wall

Step 1:
Holding inner and outer trim wrong sides together with wall between, with White/Silver, Whipstitch unfinished upper edges together between red arrows.

Overcast edge is not Whipstitched.

Step 2:
With White, Whipstitch unfinished side edges together.

iving Room

Fashion Doll Dream Castle

Study

Imagine a cozy fire in each richly appointed room. Elegant rugs and gilded frames add warmth and sparkle to your fantasy home.

BASE
CUTTING & ASSEMBLY INSTRUCTIONS:
Follow Dining Room Base Cutting & Assembly Instructions on page 20.

FIREPLACE
CUTTING INSTRUCTIONS:
Using Bedroom Mantel Front graph on page 44 for E, follow Dining Room Fireplace Cutting Instructions on page 24.

STITCHING INSTRUCTIONS:
NOTES: B and C pieces are unworked. Substitute White/Gold for White/Silver throughout.
1: Substituting Peach for Aqua on G piece, using colors and stitches indicated, work A, D, E (use Bedroom E graph), F and G pieces according to graphs. With White, Overcast F and G as indicated on graphs.
2: With thread, sew eight gold 3-mm. beads to each candlestick according to Candlestick Diagram on page 26.
3: Follow Steps 3 and 4 of Dining Room Fireplace Stitching Instructions on page 24.

HUTCH
CUTTING INSTRUCTIONS:
NOTE: Use stiff canvas throughout.
A: For interior wall pieces, cut two 16 x 90 holes, two 11 x 90 holes and one 12 x 90 holes (no graphs).
B: For vertical supports, cut four 3 x 90 holes (no graph).
C: For horizontal supports, cut six 3 x 11 holes (no graph).
D: For shelves, cut two according to Dining Room Hutch D graph on page 28.
E: For front, cut one according to graph.
F: For drawer facade, cut one 7 x 23 holes.
G: For left and right door facades, cut one each 10 x 20 holes.

STITCHING INSTRUCTIONS:
NOTE: B and C pieces are unworked.
1: Using White and stitches indicated, work A pieces according to

Dining Room Hutch A graphs on page 27. Using colors and stitches indicated, work D and E pieces according to graphs. With White, Overcast unfinished edges of E as indicated and unworked F and G pieces. Holding facades to E as indicated and working through both thicknesses as one, using colors and stitches indicated, work F and G pieces according to facade graphs.
2: With thread, sew one 5-mm. gold bead to each facade as indicated on graphs.
3: With White, Whipstitch A-C pieces together according to Steps 1-3 of Fireplace Assembly Diagram on page 25. Whipstitch D pieces to interior walls according to Dining Room Hutch Assembly Diagram on page 28.
Set pieces aside.

E – Living Room Hutch Front
(cut 1) 29 x 84 holes
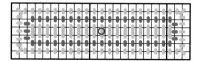

LIVING ROOM COLOR KEY:
Metallic cord
■ White/Gold
Nylon Plus™ Needloft™ yarn
□ #01   #41 White

STITCH KEY:
□ Shelf Attachment
□ Door/Drawer Attachment
○ Bead/Handle Attachment

F – Living Room Hutch Drawer Facade
(cut 1) 7 x 23 holes

G – Living Room Hutch Left Door Facade
(cut 1) 10 x 20 holes

G – Living Room Hutch Right Door Facade
(cut 1) 10 x 20 holes

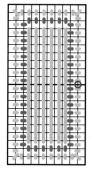

LIVING ROOM INTERIOR

WALL SUPPORT PIECES CUTTING INSTRUCTIONS:

Follow Dining Room Interior Wall Support Pieces Cutting Instructions on page 29.

INTERIOR CUTTING INSTRUCTIONS:

NOTE: Use stiff canvas throughout.

A-G: Using Living Room Floor E graphs on pages 60 and 61, follow Steps A-G of Dining Room Interior Cutting Instructions on page 29.

STITCHING INSTRUCTIONS:

NOTE: Wall support pieces are unworked.

1: Substituting White/Gold for White/Silver, Peach for Aqua and working Living Room Wall Motif on page 61 in place of Dining Room Motif, work interior A-C pieces according to graphs.

2: With White/Gold, Overcast inner cutout edges of F. Holding frame and door wall together as indicated on graph with G between, Whipstitch unfinished outer edges of F to C; working through both thicknesses, work Long Stitch at top of frame according to graph.

3: Follow Steps 2-5 of Dining Room Interior Stitching Instructions on page 29.

4: With White, Whipstitch fireplace and hutch interiors and walls to base as indicated on base graphs on pages 22 and 23 (see Wall Attachment Key on page 22) and according to Living Room Interior Assembly Diagram. Place floor inside assembly; with colors to match floor, Whipstitch floor to fireplace, hutch and walls as indicated and to bottom edges of door arch.

5: With White, Whipstitch fireplace pieces and walls together as indicated and according to Fireplace & Wall Assembly Diagram on page 35; Whipstitch hutch pieces and walls together according to Living Room Hutch & Wall Assembly Diagram.

Set aside.

Living Room Hutch & Wall Assembly Diagram

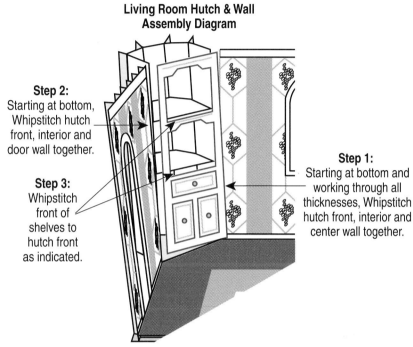

Step 2: Starting at bottom, Whipstitch hutch front, interior and door wall together.

Step 3: Whipstitch front of shelves to hutch front as indicated.

Step 1: Starting at bottom and working through all thicknesses, Whipstitch hutch front, interior and center wall together.

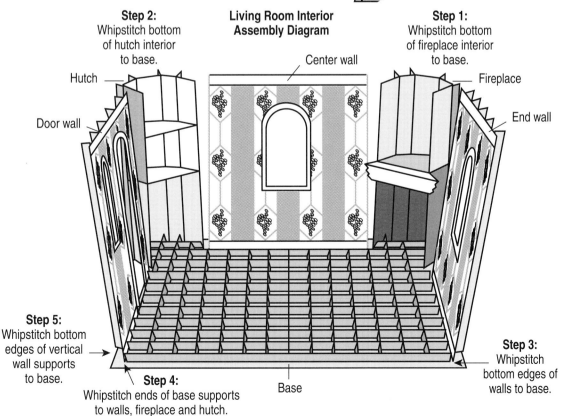

Living Room Interior Assembly Diagram

Step 2: Whipstitch bottom of hutch interior to base.

Step 1: Whipstitch bottom of fireplace interior to base.

Hutch

Door wall

Center wall

Fireplace

End wall

Step 5: Whipstitch bottom edges of vertical wall supports to base.

Step 4: Whipstitch ends of base supports to walls, fireplace and hutch.

Base

Step 3: Whipstitch bottom edges of walls to base.

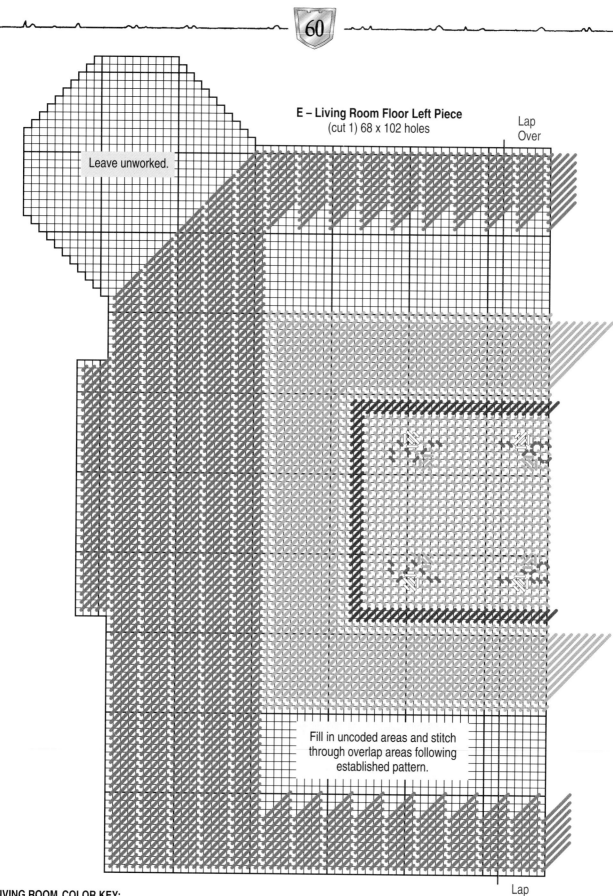

E – Living Room Floor Left Piece
(cut 1) 68 x 102 holes

Lap
Over

Leave unworked.

Fill in uncoded areas and stitch
through overlap areas following
established pattern.

Lap
Over

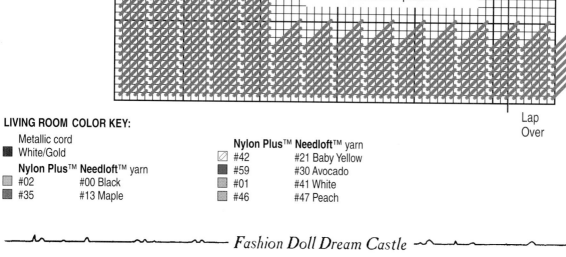

LIVING ROOM COLOR KEY:

Metallic cord
White/Gold

Nylon Plus™ Needloft™ yarn

	#02	#00 Black		
	#35	#13 Maple		

Nylon Plus™ Needloft™ yarn

#42	#21 Baby Yellow
#59	#30 Avocado
#01	#41 White
#46	#47 Peach

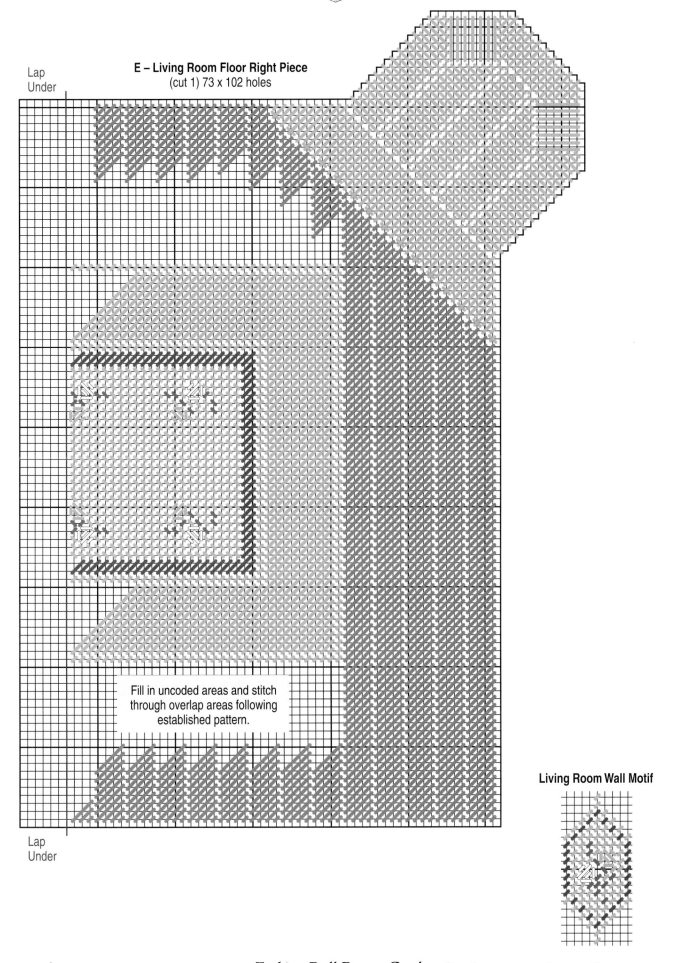

E – Living Room Floor Right Piece
(cut 1) 73 x 102 holes

Lap
Under

Fill in uncoded areas and stitch
through overlap areas following
established pattern.

Lap
Under

Living Room Wall Motif

LOWER EXTERIOR

CUTTING INSTRUCTIONS:
Follow Dining Room/Bedroom
Lower Exterior Cutting Instructions
on page 39.

STITCHING INSTRUCTIONS:
Using Living Room/Study Lower
Exterior Assembly Diagram below,
follow Dining Room/Bedroom
Lower Exterior Stitching Instruc-
tions on page 39.

**Living Room/Study
Lower Exterior
Assembly Diagram**

Whipstitch with
matching colors.

Whipstitch with
matching colors.

Whipstitch
with White.

A   C C C C C   A   C C   C C C   B

Whipstitch
with White.

Turn these pieces
to position brick pattern
as shown.

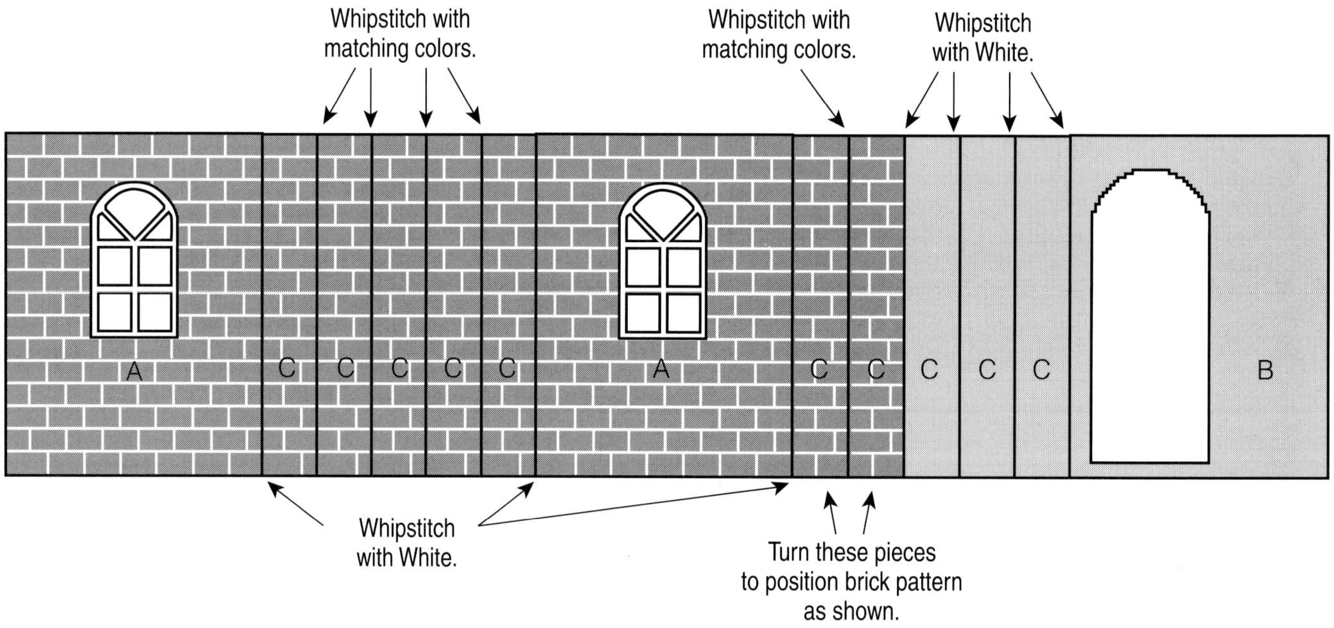

Study

BASE
CUTTING & ASSEMBLY INSTRUCTIONS:
Follow Cutting & Assembly Instructions for Dining Room Base on page 20.

For lower floor ceiling, after base is completed, using bottom of base as a pattern, cut one from felt ⅛" smaller at all edges. Glue felt to bottom of base; leaving outer ¾" unattached.

Set aside.

FIREPLACE
CUTTING INSTRUCTIONS:
Using Bedroom Mantel Front graph on page 44 for E, follow Dining Room Fireplace Cutting Instructions on page 24.

STITCHING INSTRUCTIONS:
NOTE: B and C pieces are unworked.

1: Substituting Camel for White on D-F pieces, White/Gold for White/Silver throughout and Mint for Aqua on G, work A, D, E (use Bedroom E graph), F and G pieces according to graphs.

2: With thread, sew eight gold 3-mm. beads to each candlestick according to Candlestick Diagram on page 26.

3: Substituting White/Gold for White/Silver and Camel for White, follow Steps 3 and 4 of Dining Room Fireplace Stitching Instructions on page 24.

Set aside.

CLOSET
CUTTING INSTRUCTIONS:
NOTES: Graphs and diagram on pages 63-64. Use stiff canvas for A-H pieces and white canvas for I pieces.

A: For interior wall pieces, cut two 16 x 90 holes, two 11 x 90 holes and one 12 x 90 holes(see graphs).

B: For vertical supports, cut four 3 x 90 holes (no graph).

C: For horizontal supports, cut six 3 x 90 holes (no graph).

D: For shelves, cut two according to Dining Room Hutch D graph on page 28.

E: For front, cut one according to graph.

F: For upper doors, cut two 11 x 48 holes.

G: For lower doors, cut two 11 x 18 holes.

H: For drawer facades, cut two 6 x 11 holes.

I: For handles, cut six from white according to graph.

STITCHING INSTRUCTIONS:
NOTE: A-D and I pieces are unworked.

1: Using Camel and stitches indicated, work E, F and G pieces according to graphs; Overcast unfinished edges of unworked H pieces. Holding facades to E as indicated on graph and working through both thicknesses as one, using colors and stitches indicated, work H pieces according to facade graph.

2: Overcast unfinished edges of E, outside edges of F and G pieces as indicated. (Cutout edges of front are unfinished.) Turning one of each door, Whipstitch unfinished edges of doors to front as indicated.

NOTE: Cut tan closure into four ¼" x 1" pieces.

3: Sew or glue sticky side of closures to front as indicated; cutting each fuzzy side in half, attach to corresponding areas on inside of doors.

4: For handles, with White/Gold, sew one 5-mm. gold bead and one I piece to each door and drawer facade as indicated and according to Study Closet Handle Assembly Diagram.

5: With Camel, Whipstitch A-C pieces together according to Steps 1-3 of Dining Room Fireplace Assembly Diagram. Whipstitch D pieces according to Dining Room Hutch Assembly Diagram on page 28.

Set pieces aside.

A – Study Closet Interior Wall #1 (cut 2) 16 x 90 holes

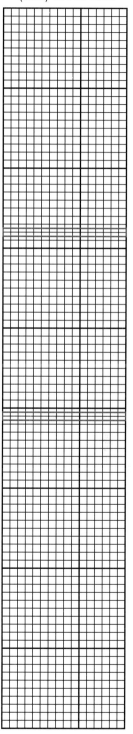

STUDY STITCH KEY:
☐ Shelf Attachment

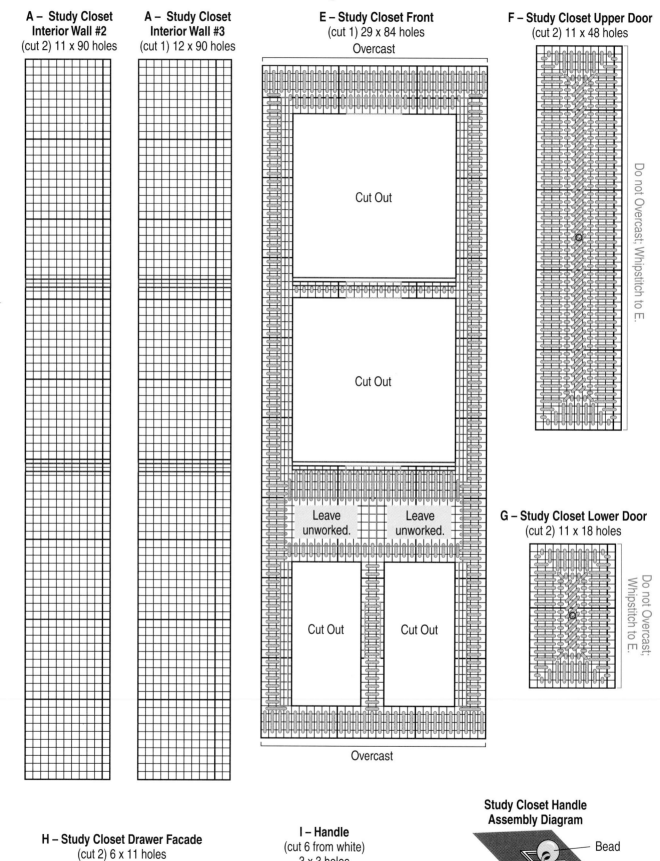

A – Study Closet Interior Wall #2
(cut 2) 11 x 90 holes

A – Study Closet Interior Wall #3
(cut 1) 12 x 90 holes

E – Study Closet Front
(cut 1) 29 x 84 holes

Overcast

Cut Out

Cut Out

Leave unworked.

Leave unworked.

Cut Out

Cut Out

Overcast

F – Study Closet Upper Door
(cut 2) 11 x 48 holes

Do not Overcast; Whipstitch to E.

G – Study Closet Lower Door
(cut 2) 11 x 18 holes

Do not Overcast; Whipstitch to E.

H – Study Closet Drawer Facade
(cut 2) 6 x 11 holes

I – Handle
(cut 6 from white)
3 x 3 holes

Study Closet Handle Assembly Diagram

Bead

Handle

STUDY INTERIOR

WALL SUPPORT PIECES CUTTING INSTRUCTIONS:

Follow Dining Room Interior Wall Support Pieces Cutting Instructions on page 29.

INTERIOR CUTTING INSTRUCTIONS:

A-G: Follow Steps A-G of Dining Room Interior Cutting Instructions on page 29.

STITCHING INSTRUCTIONS:

NOTE: Wall support pieces are unworked.

1: Substituting White/Gold for White/Silver, Baby Green for Aqua and working Study Wall Motif in place of Dining Room Motif, work interior A-C pieces according to graphs.

2: Follow Step 2 of Living Room Interior Stitching Instructions on page 59.

3: Omitting rug from floor, follow Steps 2-5 of Dining Room Interior Stitching Instructions on page 29.

4: Substituting Study Closet interior for Living Room Hutch interior, follow Step 4 of Living Room Interior Stitching Instructions on page 59.

5: With White, Whipstitch fireplace pieces and walls together according to Fireplace & Wall Assembly Diagram on page 35; substituting closet front for hutch front, Whipstitch closet pieces and walls together according to Living Room Hutch & Wall Assembly Diagram on page 59.

Set aside.

UPPER EXTERIOR

CUTTING & STITCHING INSTRUCTIONS:

Reversing placement of walls and turrets, follow Dining Room/Bedroom Upper Exterior Cutting & Stitching Instructions on page 46.

FINISHING

CUTTING INSTRUCTIONS:

Using Living Room/Study Center Turret Inner Trim graphs #1, #2, and #3 below for E pieces, follow Dining Room/Bedroom Finishing Cutting Instructions on page 51.

STITCHING INSTRUCTIONS:

Reversing direction of Overcast edges on C pieces according to Wall Trim Illustration below, follow Dining Room/Bedroom Finishing Stitching Instructions on page 51.

E – Center Turret Inner Trim #1
(cut 1) 14 x 29 holes

E – Center Turret Inner Trim #2
(cut 3) 13 x 29 holes

E – Center Turret Inner Trim #3
(cut 1) 14 x 29 holes

Overcast with White.

STUDY COLOR KEY:

Metallic cord
■ White/Gold

Nylon Plus™ Needloft™ yarn
□ #28	#26 Baby Green
■ #38	#34 Cerulean
▨ #23	#38 Gray
□ #01	#41 White
▨ #34	#43 Camel
■ #08	#50 Teal Blue

STITCH KEY:

□ Shelf Attachment
□ Door/Drawer Attachment
O Bead/Handle Attachment
□ Closure Placement

Study Wall Motif

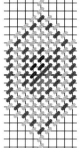

Wall Trim Illustration

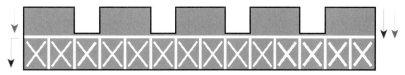

Overcast between red arrows for piece #1.
Overcast between green arrows for piece #2.

itchen

Bathroom

itchen

BASE

CUTTING INSTRUCTIONS:

NOTES: Graphs and diagram on pages 68-71. Use stiff canvas throughout.

A: For base front and back pieces, cut one each according to graphs.

B-E: For vertical base support pieces, cut number indicated according to graphs.

F-M: For horizontal base support pieces, cut number indicated according to graphs.

N: For base end pieces, cut two 5 x 5 holes, two 5 x 20 holes, two 5 x 28 holes and one 5 x 52 holes (no graphs).

STITCHING & ASSEMBLY INSTRUCTIONS:

NOTE: A-M and 5 x 5-hole N pieces are unworked.

1: Using Maple and Slanted Gobelin Stitch over narrow width, work N pieces.

2: With White, assemble pieces as indicated on graphs and according to Lower Base Assembly Diagram.

Set aside.

BASE SUPPORT COLOR CODING KEY:

- B – Vertical Base Support
- C – Vertical Base Support
- D – Vertical Base Support
- E – Vertical Base Support
- F – Horizontal Base Support
- G – Horizontal Base Support
- H – Horizontal Base Support
- I – Horizontal Base Support
- J – Horizontal Base Support
- K – Horizontal Base Support
- L – Horizontal Base Support
- M – Horizontal Base Support

Lower Base Assembly Diagram

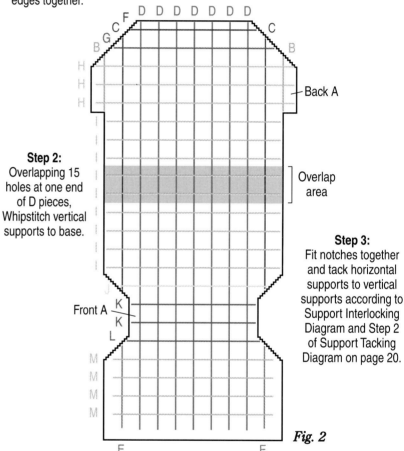

Step 1: Overlapping 16 holes on each base piece, Whipstitch edges together.

Fig. 1

Step 2: Overlapping 15 holes at one end of D pieces, Whipstitch vertical supports to base.

Step 3: Fit notches together and tack horizontal supports to vertical supports according to Support Interlocking Diagram and Step 2 of Support Tacking Diagram on page 20.

Fig. 2

Step 4: With Maple, Whipstitch N pieces and base together.

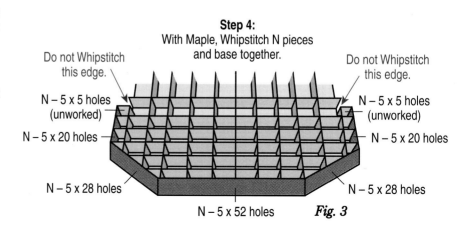

Do not Whipstitch this edge.
N – 5 x 5 holes (unworked)
N – 5 x 20 holes
N – 5 x 28 holes
N – 5 x 52 holes
Do not Whipstitch this edge.
N – 5 x 5 holes (unworked)
N – 5 x 20 holes
N – 5 x 28 holes

Fig. 3

C – Vertical Base Support
(cut 2) 4 x 111 holes

E – Vertical Base Support
(cut 2)
4 x 38 holes

D 1 – Vertical Base Support
(cut 7)
4 x 94 holes

I – Horizontal Base Support
(cut 9)
4 x 79 holes

K – Horizontal Base Support
(cut 2)
4 x 57 holes

M – Horizontal Base Support
(cut 4)
4 x 71 holes

G – Horizontal Base Support
(cut 1)
4 x 75 holes

D 2 – Vertical Base Support
(cut 7)
4 x 99 holes

H – Horizontal Base Support
(cut 3)
4 x 91 holes

J – Horizontal Base Support
(cut 1)
4 x 69 holes

L – Horizontal Base Support
(cut 1)
4 x 63 holes

Lap Under D1

F – Horizontal Base Support
(cut 1)
4 x 59 holes

Lap Over D2

B – Vertical Base Support
(cut 2)
4 x 25 holes

BASE SUPPORT COLOR CODING KEY:

- B – Vertical Base Support
- C – Vertical Base Support
- D – Vertical Base Support
- E – Vertical Base Support
- F – Horizontal Base Support
- G – Horizontal Base Support
- H – Horizontal Base Support
- I – Horizontal Base Support
- J – Horizontal Base Support
- K – Horizontal Base Support
- L – Horizontal Base Support
- M – Horizontal Base Support

WALL ATTACHMENT KEY:

- ☐ Entrance Interior Front Wall Attachment
- Entrance Interior Side Wall Attachment

A – Base Back
(cut 1) 79 x 92 holes

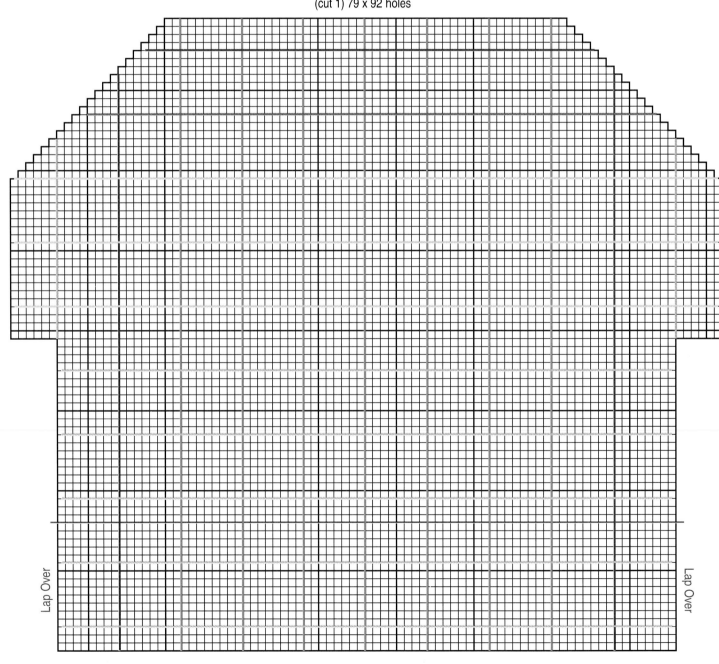

Lap Over

Lap Over

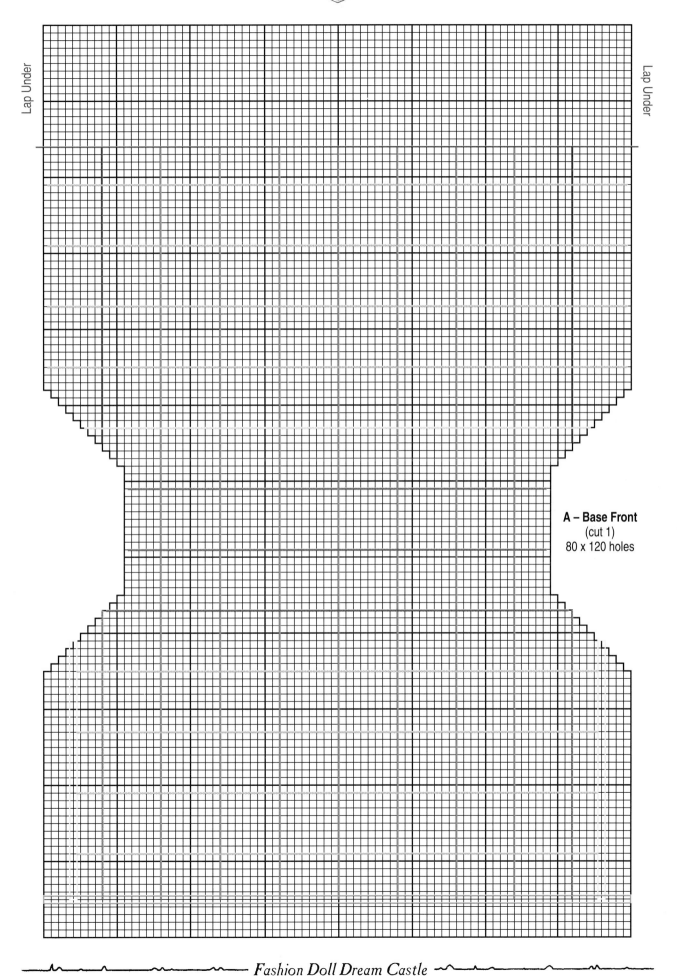

Lap Under

Lap Under

A – Base Front
(cut 1)
80 x 120 holes

ENTRANCE INTERIOR, FOYER & KITCHEN WALLS

WALL SUPPORT PIECES
CUTTING INSTRUCTIONS:

NOTES: Graphs on page 73. Use stiff canvas throughout.

A-F: For vertical support pieces, cut number indicated according to graphs.

G-O: For horizontal support pieces, cut number indicated according to graphs.

WALLS
CUTTING INSTRUCTIONS:

NOTES: Graphs and diagrams on page 72 and pages 76-81. Use stiff canvas throughout.

A: For entrance interior front wall, cut one according to graph.

B: For entrance interior right side wall, cut one 35 x 90 holes.

C: For entrance interior left side wall, cut one 35 x 90 holes.

D: For entrance right corner wall, cut one 15 x 90 holes.

E: For entrance left corner wall, cut one 15 x 90 holes.

F: For entrance/foyer right wall, cut one 15 x 90 holes.

G: For entrance/foyer left wall, cut one 15 x 90 holes.

H: For foyer right corner wall, cut one 15 x 90 holes.

I: For foyer left corner wall, cut one 15 x 90 holes.

J: For foyer/kitchen right side wall, cut one according to graph.

K: For foyer/kitchen left side wall, cut one according to graph.

L: For entrance door arch pieces, cut two 3 x 90 holes (no graph).

STITCHING INSTRUCTIONS:

NOTE: Wall support pieces are unworked.

1: Using colors and stitches indicated, work entrance and side wall A-K pieces according to graphs. Overlapping three holes at one end and working through both thicknesses at overlap area to join, using White and Slanted Gobelin Stitch over narrow width, work L pieces. With White, Overcast cutout edges of J and K pieces and side edge of K as indicated on graphs.

2: With White, Whipstitch door arch to wrong side of A as indicated. Whipstitch vertical wall supports to A-C pieces (see Exterior Wall Support Attachment Diagram) according to Entrance Interior Wall Support Assembly Illustrations.

3: Fit notches together and tack horizontal supports to vertical supports (see Support Interlocking Diagram and Step 2 of Support Tacking Diagram on page 20) according to illustrations. (**NOTE:** Remaining supports will be used later for Door Walls.)

4: With White, Whipstitch A-C pieces and base together as indicated and according to Entrance Interior Assembly Diagram on page 81.

5: With indicated colors, Whipstitch pieces together according to Wall Assembly Diagram on page 81.

Set aside.

Exterior Wall Support Attachment Diagram
(wrong side view)

With White, Whipstitch vertical supports to exterior wall at unworked areas to complete brick pattern.

Unworked area

Unworked area

A – Vertical Wall Support
(cut 10)
3 x 90 holes
Top

B – Vertical Wall Support
(cut 2)
3 x 13 holes
Top

C – Vertical Wall Support
(cut 4)
3 x 9 holes
Top

E – Vertical Wall Support
(cut 4)
3 x 17 holes
Top

F – Vertical Wall Support
(cut 2)
3 x 9 holes
Top

D – Vertical Wall Support
(cut 8)
3 x 85 holes
Top

G – Horizontal Wall Support
(cut 2)
3 x 79 holes

H – Horizontal Wall Support
(cut 2)
3 x 21 holes

K – Horizontal Wall Support
(cut 1)
3 x 57 holes

I – Horizontal Wall Support
(cut 10)
3 x 17 holes

J – Horizontal Wall Support
(cut 14)
3 x 33 holes

L – Horizontal Wall Support
(cut 2)
3 x 14 holes

M – Horizontal Wall Support
(cut 10)
3 x 12 holes

N – Horizontal Wall Support
(cut 10)
3 x 23 holes

O – Horizontal Wall Support
(cut 2)
3 x 24 holes

WALL SUPPORT COLOR CODING KEY:
- A – Vertical Wall Support
- B – Vertical Wall Support
- C – Vertical Wall Support
- G – Horizontal Wall Support
- H – Horizontal Wall Support
- I – Horizontal Wall Support
- J – Horizontal Wall Support

Entrance Interior Wall Support Assembly Illustrations

Entrance Interior A

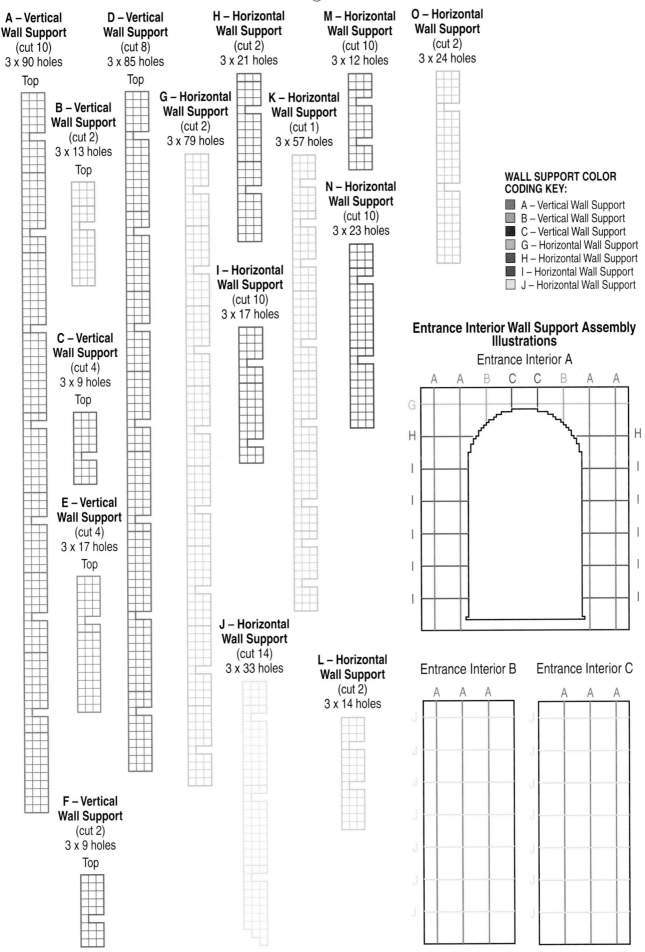

Entrance Interior B   Entrance Interior C

A – Entrance Interior Front Wall
(cut 1) 80 x 90 holes

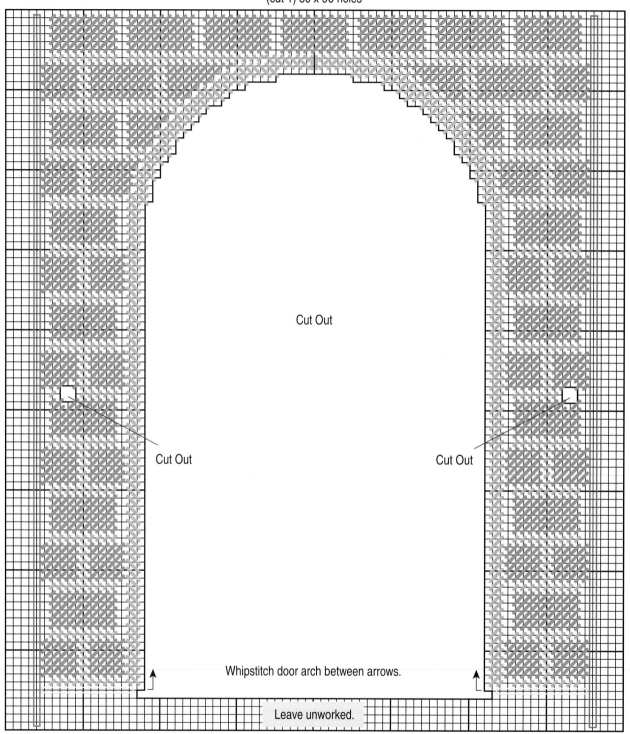

Cut Out

Cut Out

Cut Out

Whipstitch door arch between arrows.

Leave unworked.

ENTRANCE COLOR KEY:

Nylon Plus™ Needloft™ yarn

- #23   #38 Gray
- #01   #41 White

STITCH KEY:

- ☐ Wall Attachment
- ☐ Floor Attachment

B – Entrance Interior Right Side Wall
(cut 1) 35 x 90 holes

Leave unworked.

C – Entrance Interior Left Side Wall
(cut 1) 35 x 90 holes

Leave unworked.

D – Entrance Right Corner Wall (cut 1) 15 x 90 holes

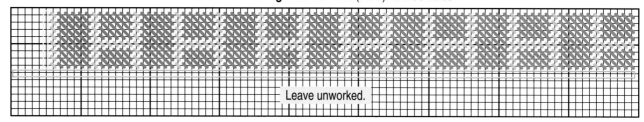

Leave unworked.

E – Entrance Left Corner Wall (cut 1) 15 x 90 holes

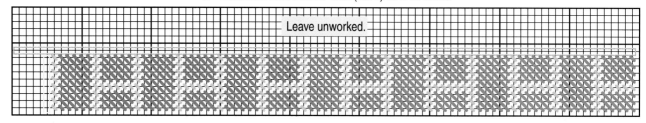

Leave unworked.

F – Entrance/Foyer Right Wall (cut 1) 15 x 90 holes

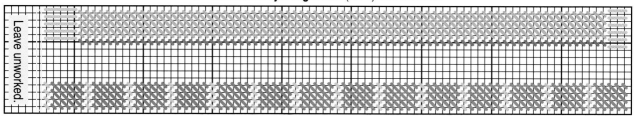

Leave unworked.

G – Entrance/Foyer Left Wall (cut 1) 15 x 90 holes

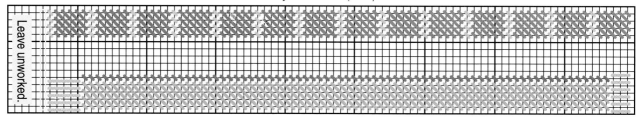

Leave unworked.

H – Foyer Right Corner Wall (cut 1) 15 x 90 holes

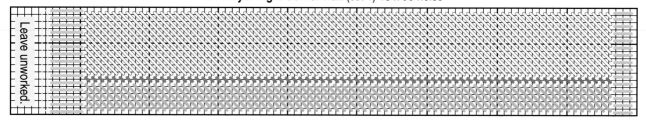

Leave unworked.

I – Foyer Left Corner Wall (cut 1) 15 x 90 holes

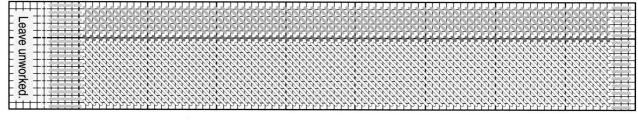

Leave unworked.

ENTRANCE COLOR KEY:

Metallic cord
■ White/Gold

Nylon Plus™ Needloft™ yarn
■ #27   #17 Gold
▨ #33   #18 Tan
▨ #42   #21 Baby Yellow
■ #23   #38 Gray

Nylon Plus™ Needloft™ yarn
□ #01   #41 White

STITCH KEY:
□ Wall Attachment
□ Shelf Attachment
Floor Attachment

J – Foyer/Kitchen Right Side Wall
(cut 1) 70 x 90 holes

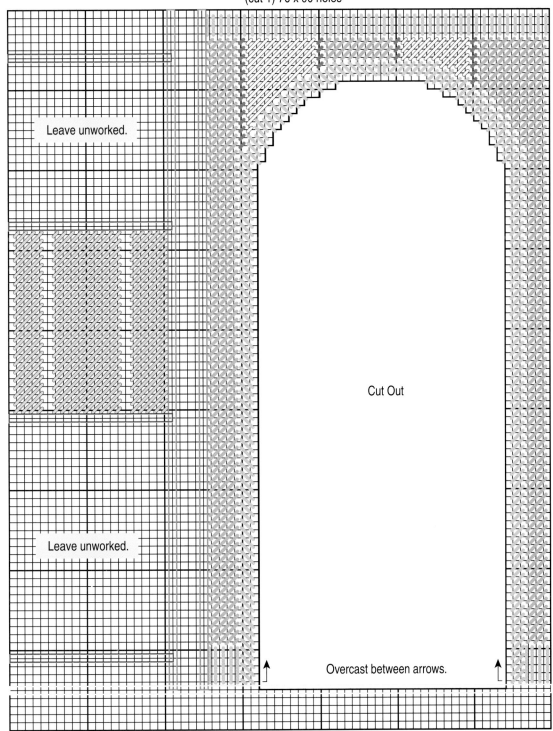

Leave unworked.

Leave unworked.

Cut Out

Overcast between arrows.

ENTRANCE COLOR KEY:

Metallic cord
■ White/Gold

Nylon Plus™ Needloft™ yarn
■ #27   #17 Gold
▨ #42   #21 Baby Yellow
☐ #30   #24 Mint
■ #01   #41 White

Nylon Plus™ Needloft™ yarn
■ #46   #47 Peach
▨ #26   #57 Yellow

STITCH KEY:
☐ Wall Attachment
  Floor Attachment

K – Foyer/Kitchen Left Side Wall
(cut 1) 70 x 90 holes

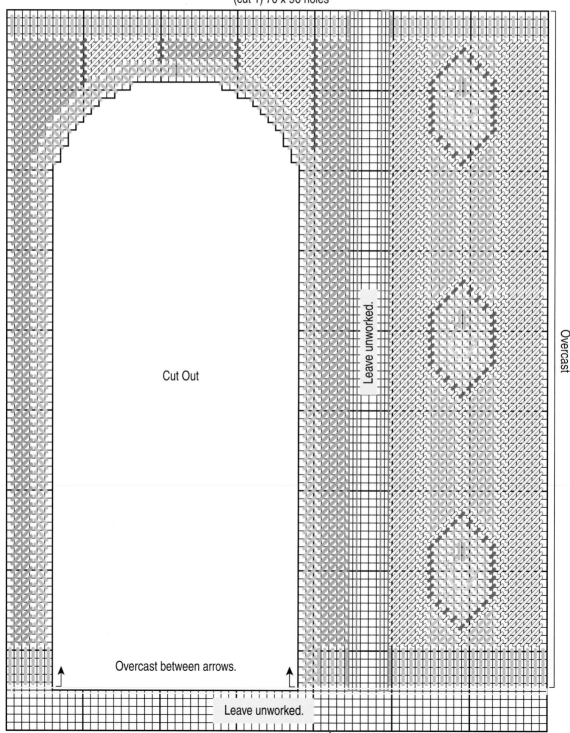

Leave unworked.

Overcast

Cut Out

Overcast between arrows.

Leave unworked.

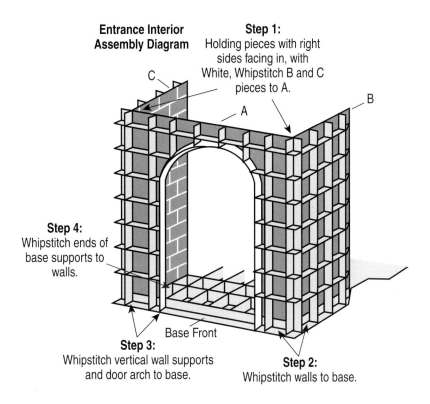

Entrance Interior Assembly Diagram

Step 1:
Holding pieces with right sides facing in, with White, Whipstitch B and C pieces to A.

Step 4:
Whipstitch ends of base supports to walls.

Base Front

Step 3:
Whipstitch vertical wall supports and door arch to base.

Step 2:
Whipstitch walls to base.

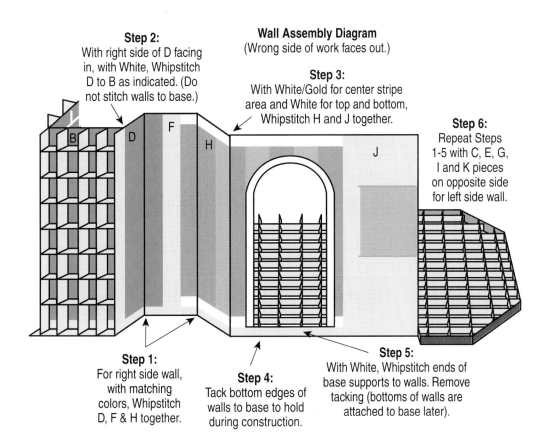

Step 2:
With right side of D facing in, with White, Whipstitch D to B as indicated. (Do not stitch walls to base.)

Wall Assembly Diagram
(Wrong side of work faces out.)

Step 3:
With White/Gold for center stripe area and White for top and bottom, Whipstitch H and J together.

Step 6:
Repeat Steps 1-5 with C, E, G, I and K pieces on opposite side for left side wall.

Step 1:
For right side wall, with matching colors, Whipstitch D, F & H together.

Step 4:
Tack bottom edges of walls to base to hold during construction.

Step 5:
With White, Whipstitch ends of base supports to walls. Remove tacking (bottoms of walls are attached to base later).

FOYER & KITCHEN DOOR WALLS & FLOOR

CUTTING INSTRUCTIONS:

NOTES: Graphs, illustrations and diagrams on pages 83-90. Use stiff canvas for A-J pieces and white canvas for K pieces.

A: For front and back floor pieces, cut one each according to graphs.

B: For entrance door wall, cut one according to graph.

C: For foyer door walls, cut one each according to graphs.

D: For kitchen door wall, cut one according to graph.

E: For door arch pieces, cut four 3 x 90 holes (no graph).

F: For kitchen cabinet front, cut one according to graph.

G: For cabinet drawer facade, cut one 7 x 23 holes.

H: For cabinet upper doors, cut two 11 x 21 holes.

I: For cabinet lower doors, cut two 11 x 18 holes.

J: For cabinet shelves, cut four according to graph.

K: For door handles, cut four from white according to graph.

STITCHING INSTRUCTIONS:

NOTE: Three J pieces and K pieces are unworked.

1: Using colors and stitches indicated, work A (overlap ends as indicated and work through both thicknesses at overlap area to join), B, C, D, H, I and one J piece according to graphs. Using White/Gold, Straight Stitch and Backstitch, embroider detail as indicated on C#2 graph. Holding drawer facade to cabinet front as indicated, with Tan, Whipstitch outside edges of G to F; working through both thicknesses as one, using stitches indicated, work F according to graph. Omitting door cutouts on cabinet front, with Tan, Overcast F, H and I pieces as indicated.

2: For handles, with White, sew one 5-mm. gold bead and one K piece to each door as indicated and according to Study Closet Handle Assembly Diagram on page 64. Turning one of each door, with Tan,

Whipstitch unfinished edges of doors to F as indicated. Whipstitch F and J pieces to D as indicated and according to Cabinet Assembly Diagram.

NOTE: Cut two ½" pieces of tan closure strip. Cut fuzzy side of each piece into two ¼" x ¾" pieces and trim each sticky piece to ⅜" x ¾".

3: Sew or glue sticky closure pieces to F as indicated and fuzzy pieces to corresponding areas on doors.

4: For each door arch, overlapping 10 holes at one end of two pieces and working through both thicknesses to join, using White and Slanted Gobelin Stitch over narrow width (see Door Arch Overlapping Diagram on page 29), work E pieces. Whipstitch one arch to wrong side of each C piece as indicated.

5: Whipstitch vertical wall supports (cut in previous section) to

B and D pieces according to Wall Support Assembly Illustrations on page 86 and Interior and Exterior Wall Support Attachment Diagrams on pages 31 and 72. Fit notches together and tack horizontal supports to vertical supports (see Support Interlocking and Tacking Diagrams on page 20).

6: With White, Whipstitch C#1 door arch to B and C#2 arch to D. Positioning C#1/B wall unit over floor as indicated, with colors to match floor, Whipstitch walls and supports to floor as indicated and according to Door Wall Assembly Diagram. Repeat with C#2/D wall unit.

7: Placing assembled walls and floor over base, with indicated colors, Whipstitch walls, shelves, floor and base together as indicated and according to Foyer/Kitchen Assembly Diagram.

Set aside.

Door Wall Assembly Diagram

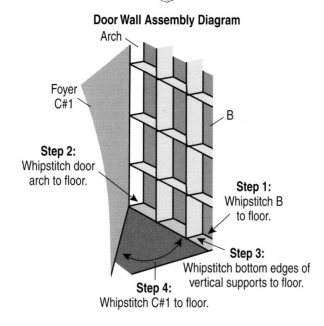

Arch

Foyer
C#1

B

Step 2:
Whipstitch door
arch to floor.

Step 1:
Whipstitch B
to floor.

Step 3:
Whipstitch bottom edges of
vertical supports to floor.

Step 4:
Whipstitch C#1 to floor.

Foyer/Kitchen Assembly Diagram

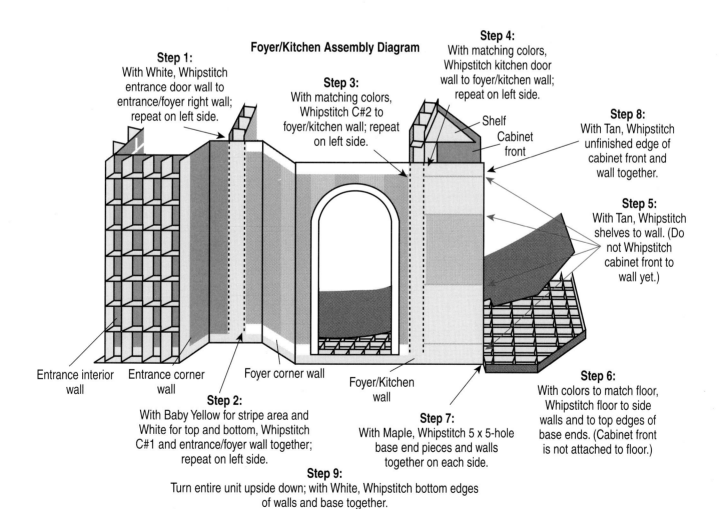

Step 1:
With White, Whipstitch
entrance door wall to
entrance/foyer right wall;
repeat on left side.

Step 3:
With matching colors,
Whipstitch C#2 to
foyer/kitchen wall; repeat
on left side.

Step 4:
With matching colors,
Whipstitch kitchen door
wall to foyer/kitchen wall;
repeat on left side.

Shelf
Cabinet
front

Step 8:
With Tan, Whipstitch
unfinished edge of
cabinet front and
wall together.

Step 5:
With Tan, Whipstitch
shelves to wall. (Do
not Whipstitch
cabinet front to
wall yet.)

Entrance interior
wall

Entrance corner
wall

Foyer corner wall

Foyer/Kitchen
wall

Step 2:
With Baby Yellow for stripe area and
White for top and bottom, Whipstitch
C#1 and entrance/foyer wall together;
repeat on left side.

Step 7:
With Maple, Whipstitch 5 x 5-hole
base end pieces and walls
together on each side.

Step 6:
With colors to match floor,
Whipstitch floor to side
walls and to top edges of
base ends. (Cabinet front
is not attached to floor.)

Step 9:
Turn entire unit upside down; with White, Whipstitch bottom edges
of walls and base together.

A – Lower Floor Back
(cut 1) 75 x 92 holes

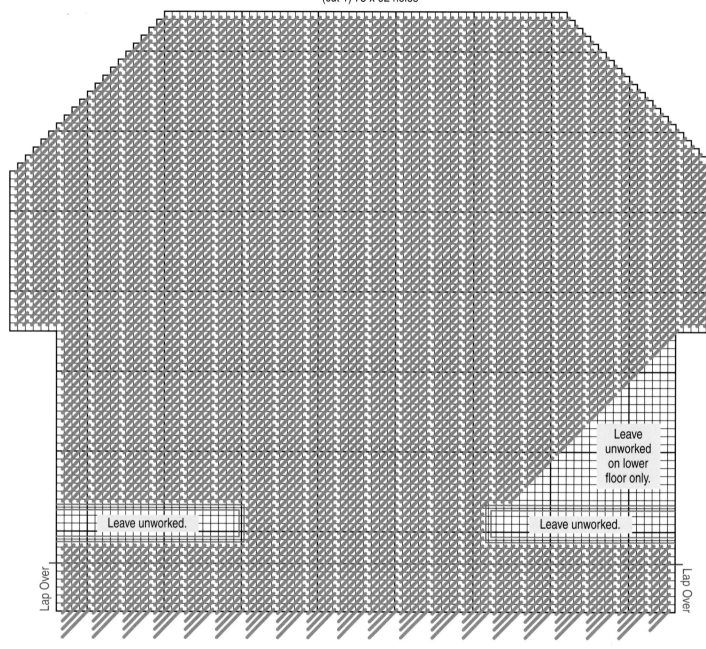

Leave unworked on lower floor only.

Leave unworked.

Leave unworked.

Lap Over

Lap Over

LOWER FLOOR COLOR KEY:

Metallic cord
☐ White/Silver
◼ White/Gold

Nylon Plus™ Needloft™ yarn
◼ #35   #13 Maple
◼ #38   #34 Cerulean
◼ #23   #38 Gray
◼ #08   #50 Teal Blue

STITCH KEY:
☐ Wall Attachment

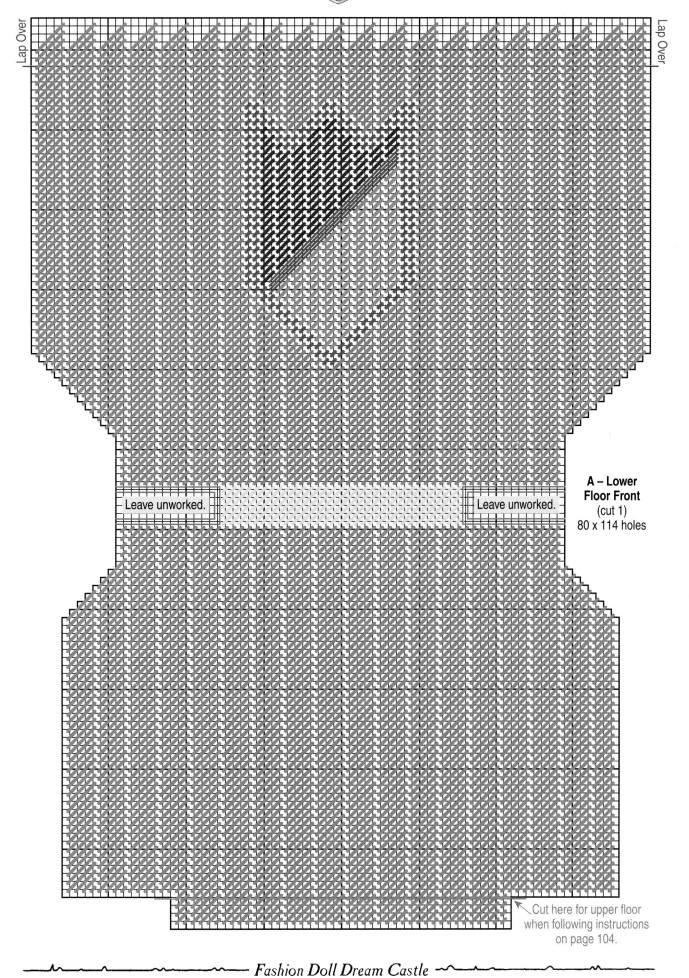

Lap Over

Lap Over

Leave unworked.

Leave unworked.

**A – Lower
Floor Front**
(cut 1)
80 x 114 holes

Cut here for upper floor
when following instructions
on page 104.

B – Entrance Door Wall
(cut 1) 58 x 85 holes

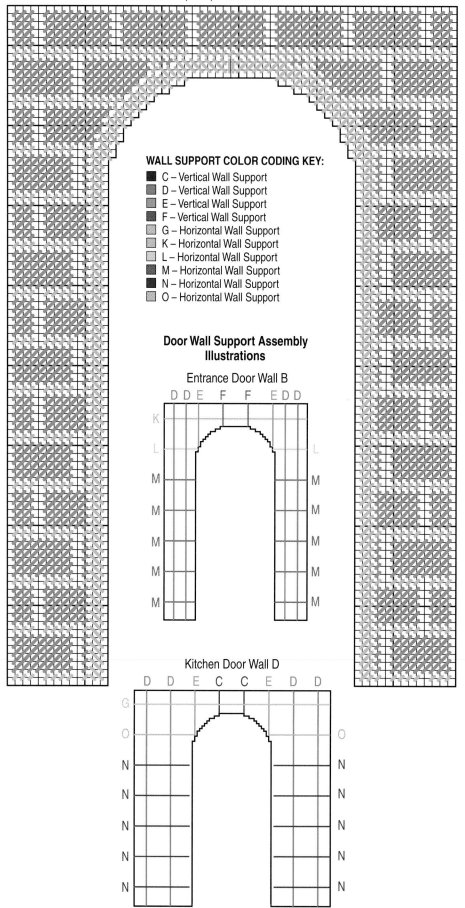

WALL SUPPORT COLOR CODING KEY:

■ C – Vertical Wall Support
■ D – Vertical Wall Support
■ E – Vertical Wall Support
■ F – Vertical Wall Support
■ G – Horizontal Wall Support
■ K – Horizontal Wall Support
■ L – Horizontal Wall Support
■ M – Horizontal Wall Support
■ N – Horizontal Wall Support
■ O – Horizontal Wall Support

Door Wall Support Assembly Illustrations

Entrance Door Wall B

Kitchen Door Wall D

C – Lower Foyer Door Wall #1
(cut 1) 58 x 85 holes

KITCHEN COLOR KEY:

Metallic cord
■ White/Gold

Nylon Plus™ Needloft™ yarn
#27	#17 Gold
#42	#21 Baby Yellow
#23	#38 Gray
#01	#41 White

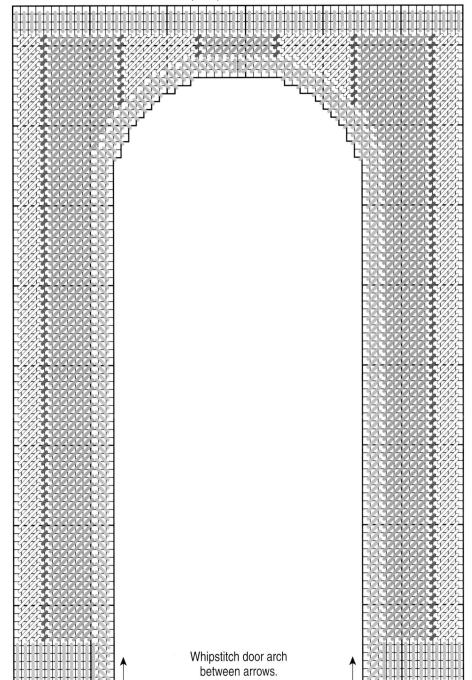

Whipstitch door arch
between arrows.

C – Lower Foyer Door Wall #2
(cut 1) 80 x 85 holes

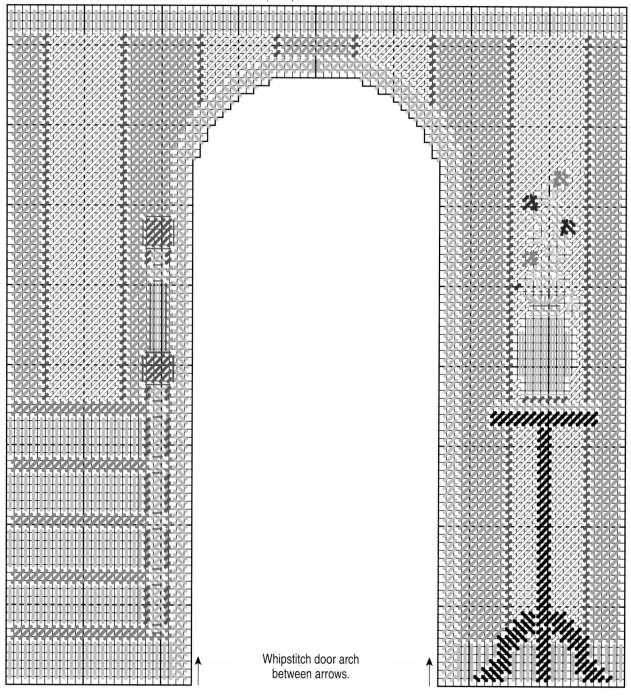

Whipstitch door arch
between arrows.

D – Kitchen Door Wall
(cut 1) 80 x 85 holes

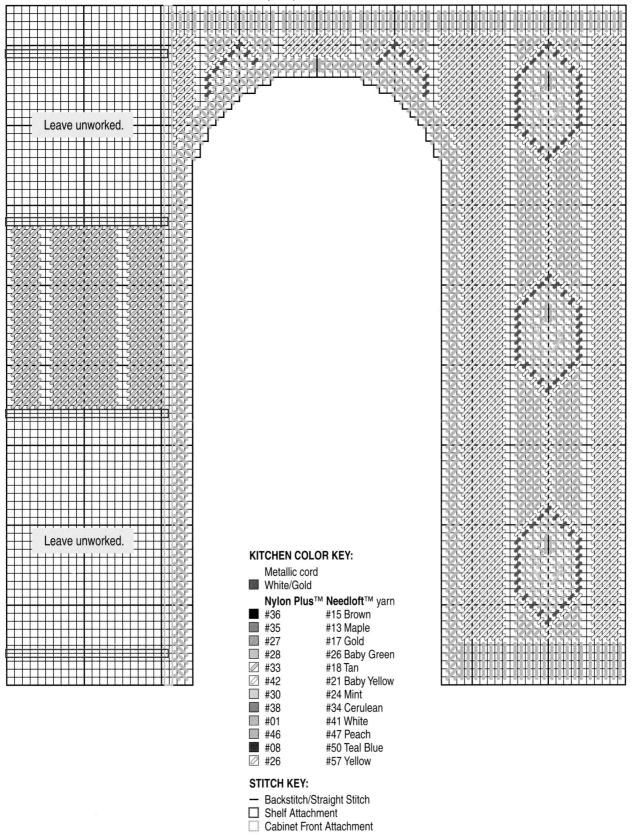

Leave unworked.

Leave unworked.

KITCHEN COLOR KEY:

Metallic cord
White/Gold

Nylon Plus™ Needloft™ yarn

■	#36		#15 Brown
	#35		#13 Maple
	#27		#17 Gold
	#28		#26 Baby Green
⊘	#33		#18 Tan
⊘	#42		#21 Baby Yellow
	#30		#24 Mint
	#38		#34 Cerulean
	#01		#41 White
	#46		#47 Peach
■	#08		#50 Teal Blue
⊘	#26		#57 Yellow

STITCH KEY:

— Backstitch/Straight Stitch
☐ Shelf Attachment
☐ Cabinet Front Attachment

F – Kitchen Cabinet Front
(cut 1) 29 x 85 holes
Overcast

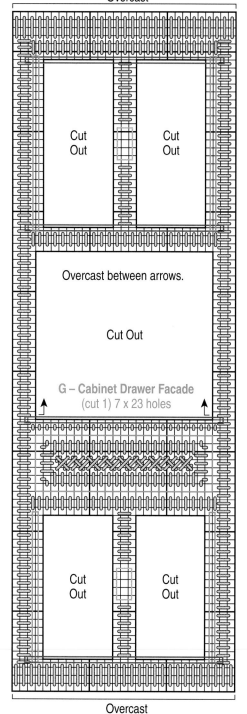

Cut Out

Cut Out

Overcast between arrows.

Cut Out

G – Cabinet Drawer Facade
(cut 1) 7 x 23 holes

Cut Out

Cut Out

Overcast

H – Cabinet Upper Door
(cut 2) 11 x 21 holes

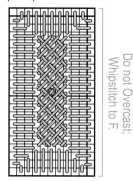

Do not Overcast; Whipstitch to F.

NOTE: Work slanted stitch areas according to Woven Stitch Illustration.

I – Cabinet Lower Door
(cut 2) 11 x 18 holes

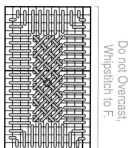

Do not Overcast; Whipstitch to F.

K – Door Handle
(cut 4 from white)
3 x 3 holes

J – Kitchen Cabinet Shelf
(cut 4) 14 x 27 holes

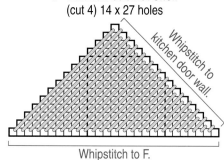

Whipstitch to kitchen door wall.

Whipstitch to F.

Woven Stitch Illustration

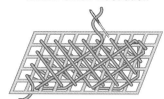

Cabinet Assembly Diagram

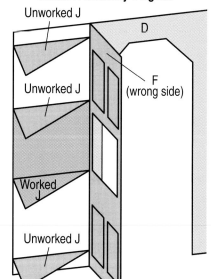

Unworked J

Unworked J

Worked J

Unworked J

D

F (wrong side)

KITCHEN COLOR KEY:
Nylon Plus™ Needloft™ yarn
▨ #33   #18 Tan

STITCH KEY:
☐ Door/Drawer Attachment
○ Bead/Handle Attachment
☐ Velcro Attachment
☐ Shelf Attachment

ENTRANCE EXTERIOR & DOORS

CUTTING INSTRUCTIONS:

NOTES: Graphs, illustration and diagrams on pages 91-95. Use stiff canvas throughout.

A: For entrance exterior front wall, cut one according to graph.

B: For entrance exterior side walls, cut two 35 x 90 holes.

C: For front door exterior and interior, cut one each according to graphs.

D: For double door sides #1 and #2, cut two each according to graphs.

E: For door hinges, cut three 3 x 34 holes (no graph).

F: For washers, cut two according to graph.

STITCHING INSTRUCTIONS:

NOTE: F pieces are unworked.

1: Using colors and stitches indicated, work A-D pieces according to graphs. (**NOTE:** If desired, Slanted Gobelin Stitch over four bars may be substituted for Special Sheaf Stitch on doors.) Using White and Slanted Gobelin Stitch over narrow width, work E pieces.

2: With indicated colors, assemble exterior according to Entrance Exterior Assembly Diagram.

3: With White, assemble entrance door according to Entrance Door Assembly Diagram; assemble double doors according to Double Door Assembly Diagram.

Set aside.

Entrance Exterior Assembly Diagram

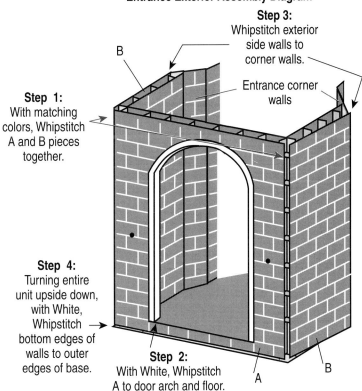

Step 1:
With matching colors, Whipstitch A and B pieces together.

Step 3:
Whipstitch exterior side walls to corner walls.

Entrance corner walls

B

Step 4:
Turning entire unit upside down, with White, Whipstitch bottom edges of walls to outer edges of base.

Step 2:
With White, Whipstitch A to door arch and floor.

A

B

Step 5:
Placing one F between screw and entrance interior wall, attach drawer pulls to front walls at cutouts.

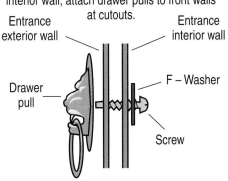

Entrance exterior wall

Entrance interior wall

Drawer pull

F – Washer

Screw

A – Entrance Exterior Front Wall
(cut 1) 80 x 90 holes

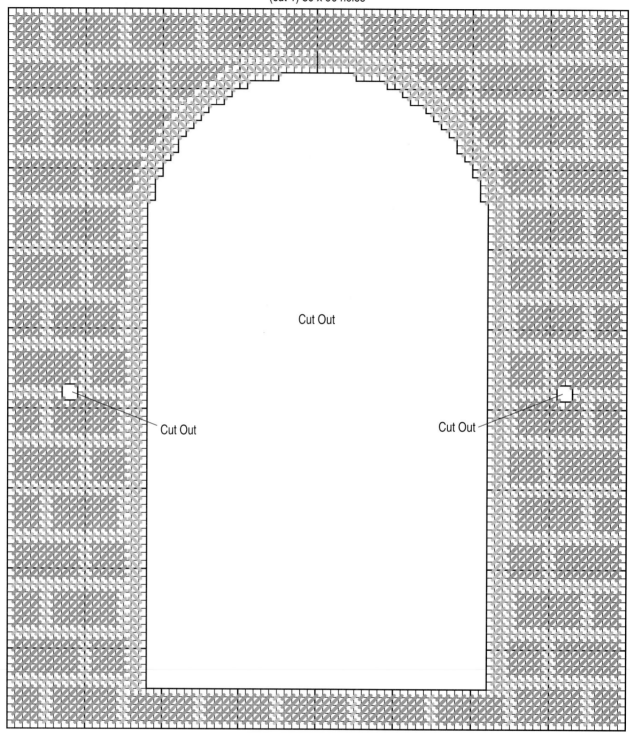

Cut Out

Cut Out

Cut Out

ENTRANCE COLOR KEY:

Nylon Plus™ Needloft™ yarn
#23   #38 Gray
#01   #41 White

B – Entrance Exterior Side Wall
(cut 2) 35 x 90 holes

C – Front Door Exterior
(cut 1) 29 x 74 holes

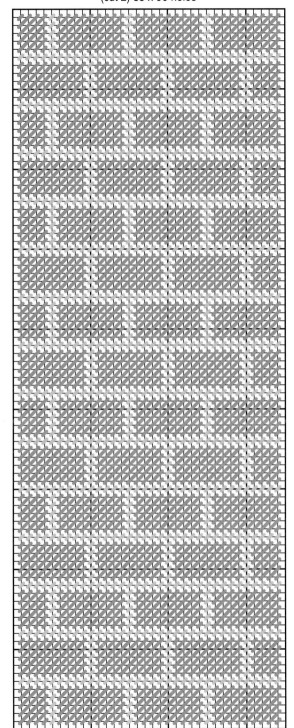

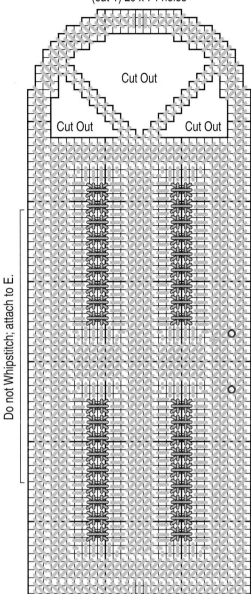

Cut Out

Cut Out

Cut Out

Do not Whipstitch; attach to E.

NOTE: Work crossed stitch areas
according to Special Sheaf Stitch Illustration.

Special Sheaf Stitch Illustration

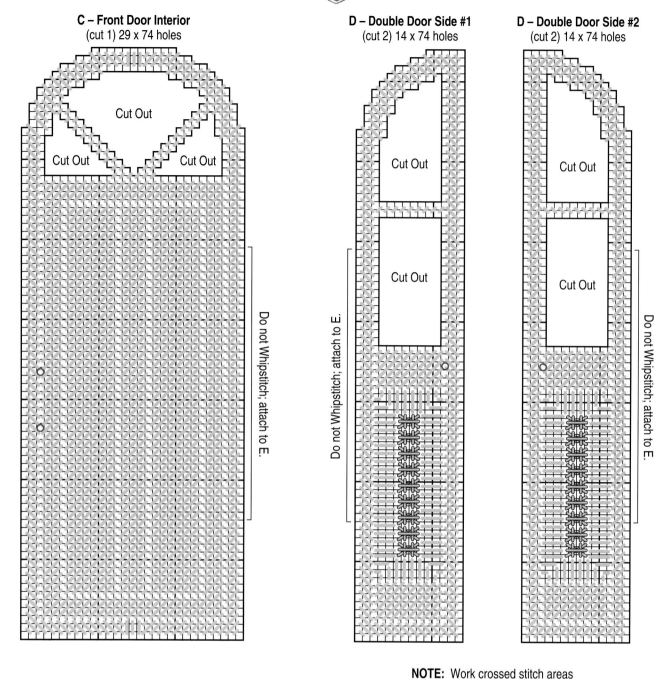

C – Front Door Interior
(cut 1) 29 x 74 holes

Cut Out

Cut Out   Cut Out

Do not Whipstitch; attach to E.

D – Double Door Side #1
(cut 2) 14 x 74 holes

Cut Out

Cut Out

Do not Whipstitch; attach to E.

D – Double Door Side #2
(cut 2) 14 x 74 holes

Cut Out

Cut Out

Do not Whipstitch; attach to E.

NOTE: Work crossed stitch areas
according to Special Sheaf Stitch Illustration on page 93.

F – Washer
(cut 2) 4 x 4 holes

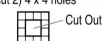 — Cut Out

ENTRANCE COLOR KEY:
Nylon Plus™ Needloft™ yarn
☐ #01   #41 White

STITCH KEY:
○ Bead/Handle Attachment

Entrance Door Assembly Diagram

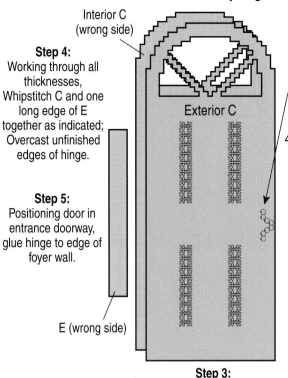

Interior C
(wrong side)

Exterior C

E (wrong side)

Step 4:
Working through all thicknesses, Whipstitch C and one long edge of E together as indicated; Overcast unfinished edges of hinge.

Step 5:
Positioning door in entrance doorway, glue hinge to edge of foyer wall.

Step 1:
Thread White through top handle attachment on exterior C as indicated on graph; thread eight silver 4-mm. beads onto yarn. Thread yarn through bottom handle attachment; pull snug and secure ends on wrong side.

Step 2:
Repeat Step 1 on interior C piece.

Step 3:
Holding C pieces wrong sides together, with White, Whipstitch together as indicated.

Berry Bead Handle Diagram

Step 1:
Gently pull berry bead apart and discard center sections.

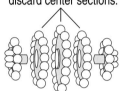

Step 2:
With White, sew one berry bead end and 4-mm. silver bead to door as indicated.

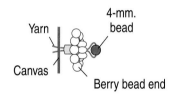

4-mm. bead

Yarn

Canvas

Berry bead end

Double Door Assembly Diagram

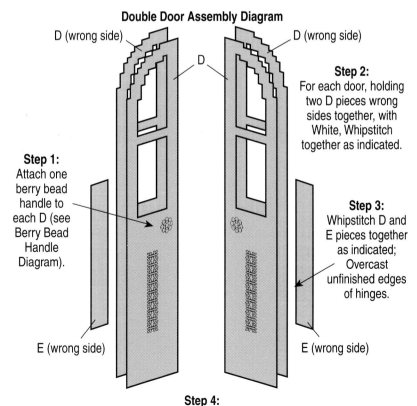

D (wrong side)

D (wrong side)

D

Step 1:
Attach one berry bead handle to each D (see Berry Bead Handle Diagram).

Step 2:
For each door, holding two D pieces wrong sides together, with White, Whipstitch together as indicated.

Step 3:
Whipstitch D and E pieces together as indicated; Overcast unfinished edges of hinges.

E (wrong side)

E (wrong side)

Step 4:
Positioning doors in kitchen doorway, glue hinges to foyer wall.

athroom

BASE

CUTTING & ASSEMBLY INSTRUCTIONS:
Follow Kitchen Base Cutting Instructions on page 68.

STITCHING & ASSEMBLY INSTRUCTIONS:
NOTE: A-M and 5 x 5-hole N pieces are unworked.
1: Using Maple and Slanted Gobelin Stitch over narrow width, work N pieces.
2: Follow Step 1 (Fig. 1) of Lower Base Assembly Diagram on page 68.
3: Follow Steps 2-4 of Upper Base Assembly Diagram on this page.
4: Follow Step 4 (Fig. 3) of Lower Base Assembly Diagram on page 68.
Set pieces aside.

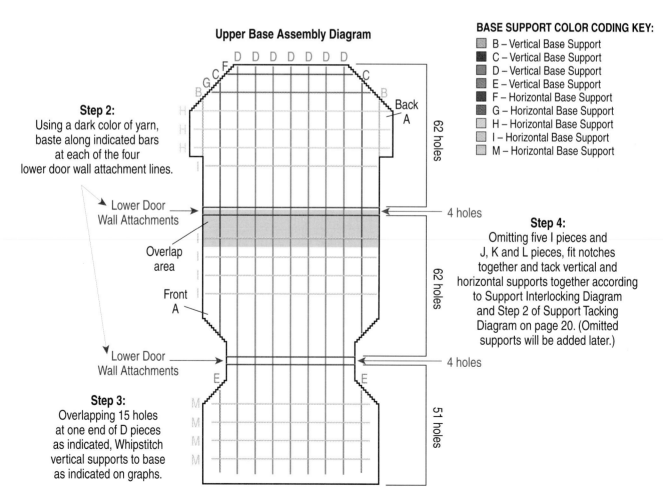

Upper Base Assembly Diagram

BASE SUPPORT COLOR CODING KEY:
- B – Vertical Base Support
- C – Vertical Base Support
- D – Vertical Base Support
- E – Vertical Base Support
- F – Horizontal Base Support
- G – Horizontal Base Support
- H – Horizontal Base Support
- I – Horizontal Base Support
- M – Horizontal Base Support

Step 2:
Using a dark color of yarn, baste along indicated bars at each of the four lower door wall attachment lines.

Lower Door Wall Attachments

Overlap area

Front A

Lower Door Wall Attachments

Back A

62 holes

4 holes

62 holes

4 holes

51 holes

Step 4:
Omitting five I pieces and J, K and L pieces, fit notches together and tack vertical and horizontal supports together according to Support Interlocking Diagram and Step 2 of Support Tacking Diagram on page 20. (Omitted supports will be added later.)

Step 3:
Overlapping 15 holes at one end of D pieces as indicated, Whipstitch vertical supports to base as indicated on graphs.

BALCONY INTERIOR, FOYER & BATHROOM WALLS

WALL SUPPORT PIECES CUTTING INSTRUCTIONS:

NOTES: Graphs on page 99. Use stiff canvas throughout.

A-E: For vertical support pieces, cut number indicated according to graphs.

F-L: For horizontal support pieces, cut number indicated according to graphs.

WALLS CUTTING INSTRUCTIONS:

NOTES: Graphs, diagrams and illustrations on pages 97-103. Use stiff canvas throughout.

A: For balcony interior front wall, cut one according to graph.

B: For balcony interior left and right walls, cut one each 35 x 36 holes.

C: For balcony corner walls, cut two according to graph.

D: For balcony/foyer right wall, cut one according to graph.

E: For balcony/foyer left wall, cut one according to graph.

F: For foyer right corner wall, cut one 15 x 90 holes.

G: For foyer left corner wall, cut one 15 x 90 holes.

H: For foyer/bathroom right side wall, cut one according to graph.

I: For foyer/bathroom left side wall, cut one according to graph.

J: For lower floor ceiling, using bottom of base as a pattern, cut one from felt ⅛" smaller at all edges.

STITCHING INSTRUCTIONS:

NOTE: Wall support pieces and balcony corner wall C pieces are unworked.

1: Using colors and stitches indicated, work A, B and D-I pieces according to graphs. With White, Overcast unfinished cutout edges of H and I pieces as indicated on graphs.

2: With White, Whipstitch vertical wall supports to A and B pieces according to Balcony Interior Wall Support Assembly Illustrations on page 99 and Exterior Wall Support Attachment Diagram on page 72.

3: Fit notches together and tack horizontal supports to vertical supports (see Support Interlocking Diagram and Step 2 of Support Tacking Diagram on page 20) according to illustrations. (**NOTE:** Remaining vertical supports will be used in door walls.)

4: With White, Whipstitch A, B pieces and base together according to Balcony Interior Assembly Diagram on this page. Glue J centered to bottom of base.

5: For side wall sections, with indicated colors, Whipstitch C-G pieces together according to Side Wall Assembly Illustrations.

6: With indicated colors, assemble pieces as indicated and according to Upper Floor Assembly Diagram. Set aside.

Balcony Interior Assembly Diagram

Step 1:
Holding pieces with right sides facing in, with White, Whipstitch A and B pieces together as indicated.

Left B

Right B

A

Base

Step 2:
Whipstitch walls to base as indicated.

Step 3:
Whipstitch ends of vertical wall supports to base.

Upper Floor Assembly Diagram
(See Figs. 2 & 3 on next page.)

Step 1:
Place balcony interior/base assembly over lower floor unit; using a sharp needle and going through felt, working along basted bars, with White, Whipstitch top edge of lower door walls to upper base. (Do not Whipstitch outer edge of base to lower walls yet.)

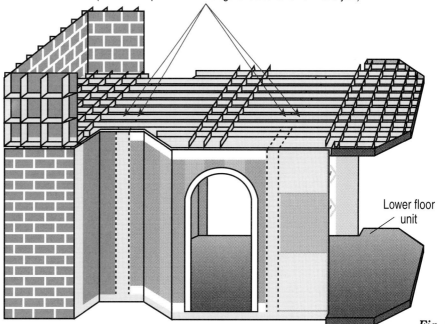

Lower floor unit

Fig. 1

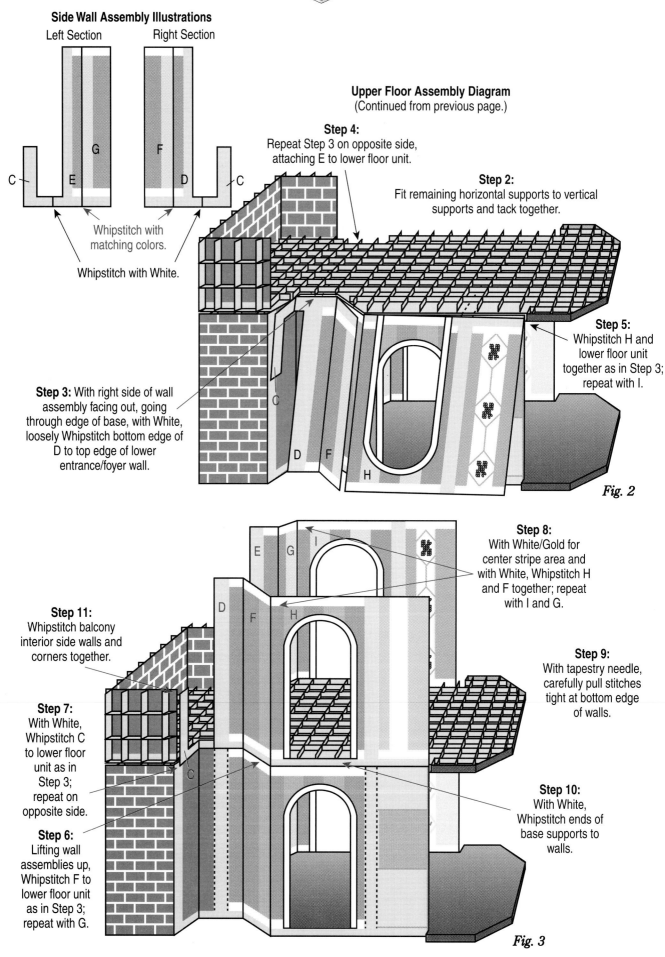

Side Wall Assembly Illustrations

Left Section   Right Section

Whipstitch with matching colors.

Whipstitch with White.

Upper Floor Assembly Diagram
(Continued from previous page.)

Step 4: Repeat Step 3 on opposite side, attaching E to lower floor unit.

Step 2: Fit remaining horizontal supports to vertical supports and tack together.

Step 5: Whipstitch H and lower floor unit together as in Step 3; repeat with I.

Step 3: With right side of wall assembly facing out, going through edge of base, with White, loosely Whipstitch bottom edge of D to top edge of lower entrance/foyer wall.

Fig. 2

Step 8: With White/Gold for center stripe area and with White, Whipstitch H and F together; repeat with I and G.

Step 11: Whipstitch balcony interior side walls and corners together.

Step 9: With tapestry needle, carefully pull stitches tight at bottom edge of walls.

Step 7: With White, Whipstitch C to lower floor unit as in Step 3; repeat on opposite side.

Step 6: Lifting wall assemblies up, Whipstitch F to lower floor unit as in Step 3; repeat with G.

Step 10: With White, Whipstitch ends of base supports to walls.

Fig. 3

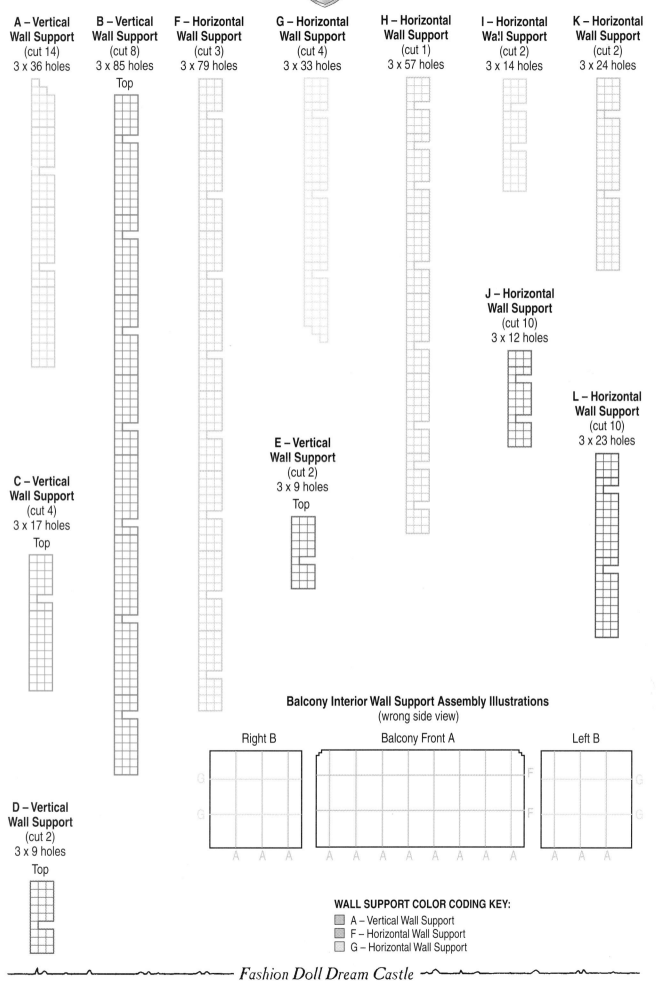

A – Vertical Wall Support
(cut 14)
3 x 36 holes

B – Vertical Wall Support
(cut 8)
3 x 85 holes
Top

F – Horizontal Wall Support
(cut 3)
3 x 79 holes

G – Horizontal Wall Support
(cut 4)
3 x 33 holes

H – Horizontal Wall Support
(cut 1)
3 x 57 holes

I – Horizontal Wall Support
(cut 2)
3 x 14 holes

K – Horizontal Wall Support
(cut 2)
3 x 24 holes

J – Horizontal Wall Support
(cut 10)
3 x 12 holes

L – Horizontal Wall Support
(cut 10)
3 x 23 holes

C – Vertical Wall Support
(cut 4)
3 x 17 holes
Top

E – Vertical Wall Support
(cut 2)
3 x 9 holes
Top

D – Vertical Wall Support
(cut 2)
3 x 9 holes
Top

Balcony Interior Wall Support Assembly Illustrations
(wrong side view)

Right B   Balcony Front A   Left B

WALL SUPPORT COLOR CODING KEY:
A – Vertical Wall Support
F – Horizontal Wall Support
G – Horizontal Wall Support

Attach support A
along entire length
of unworked bar.

Attach support A
along entire length
of unworked bar.

A – Balcony Interior Front Wall
(cut 1) 36 x 80 holes

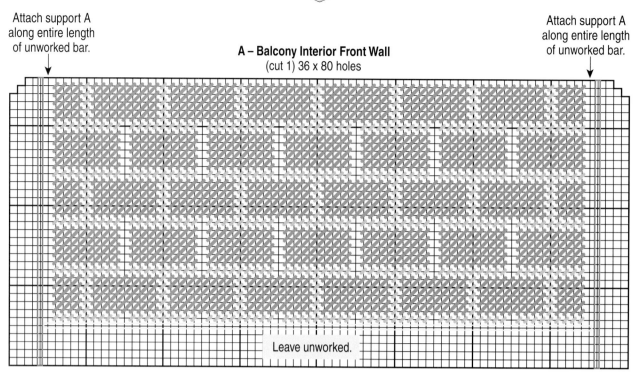

Leave unworked.

B – Balcony Interior Left Wall
(cut 1) 35 x 36 holes

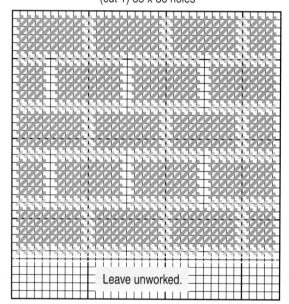

Leave unworked.

B – Balcony Interior Right Wall
(cut 1) 35 x 36 holes

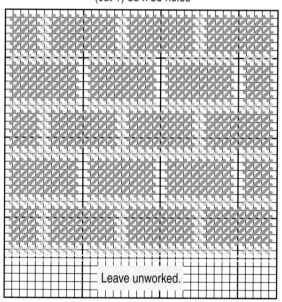

Leave unworked.

BALCONY COLOR KEY:

Metallic cord
■ White/Gold

Nylon Plus™ Needloft™ yarn
■ #27   #17 Gold
▨ #42   #21 Baby Yellow
■ #23   #38 Gray
■ #01   #41 White

STITCH KEY:
□ Wall Attachment
  Floor Attachment

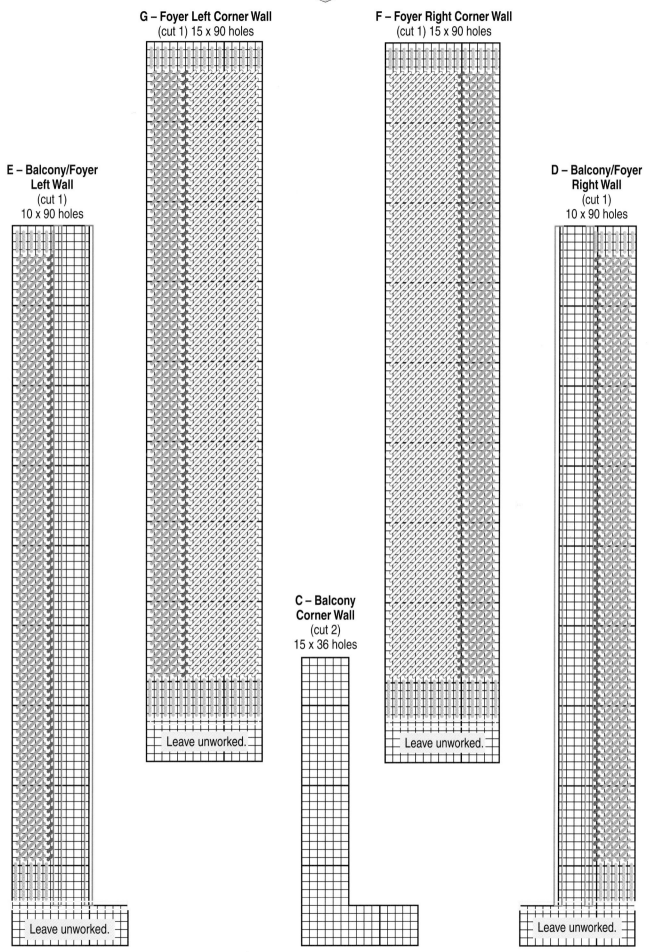

G – Foyer Left Corner Wall
(cut 1) 15 x 90 holes

F – Foyer Right Corner Wall
(cut 1) 15 x 90 holes

**E – Balcony/Foyer
Left Wall**
(cut 1)
10 x 90 holes

**D – Balcony/Foyer
Right Wall**
(cut 1)
10 x 90 holes

**C – Balcony
Corner Wall**
(cut 2)
15 x 36 holes

Leave unworked.

Leave unworked.

Leave unworked.

Leave unworked.

H – Foyer/Bathroom Right Side Wall
(cut 1) 70 x 90 holes

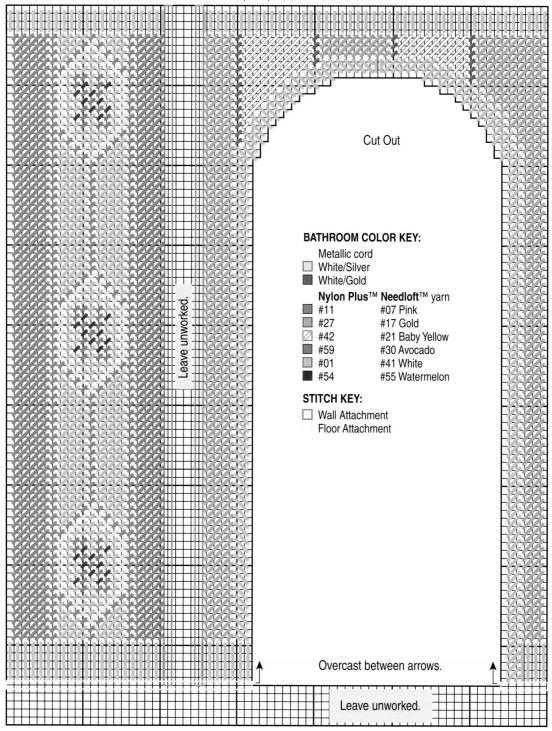

Cut Out

Leave unworked.

BATHROOM COLOR KEY:
Metallic cord
☐ White/Silver
■ White/Gold

Nylon Plus™ Needloft™ yarn
▨ #11   #07 Pink
☐ #27   #17 Gold
▨ #42   #21 Baby Yellow
▨ #59   #30 Avocado
☐ #01   #41 White
■ #54   #55 Watermelon

STITCH KEY:
☐ Wall Attachment
   Floor Attachment

↑ Overcast between arrows. ↑

Leave unworked.

I – Foyer/Bathroom Left Side Wall
(cut 1) 70 x 90 holes

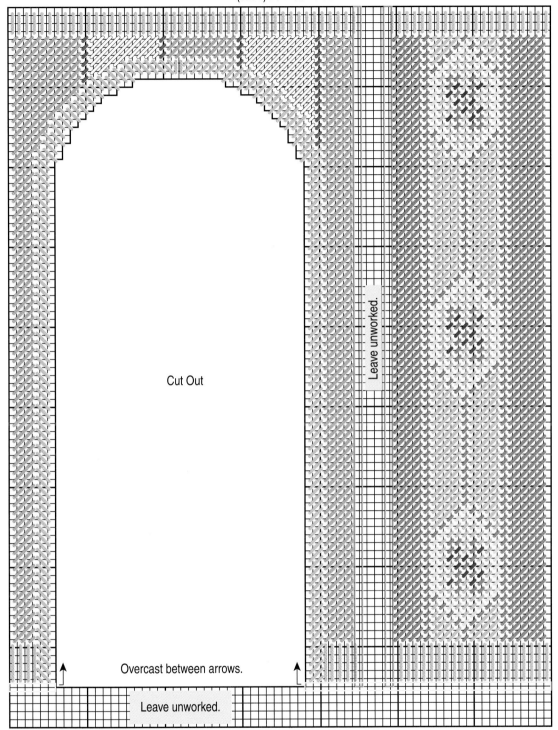

Cut Out

Leave unworked.

Overcast between arrows.

Leave unworked.

FOYER & BATHROOM DOOR WALLS & FLOOR

CUTTING INSTRUCTIONS:

A: For front and back floor pieces, cut one each according to Foyer & Kitchen Door Walls & Floor A and B graphs on pages 84-85.

B: For balcony door wall, cut one according to graph on page 105.

C: For foyer door walls, cut one according to Lower Floor Foyer Door Wall #1 graph on page 87 and one according to Upper Floor Foyer Door Wall #2 graph on page 106.

D: For bathroom door wall, cut one according to graph on page 107.

E: For door arch pieces, cut four 3 x 90 holes (no graph).

STITCHING INSTRUCTIONS:

1: Using colors and stitches indicated, work A (overlap ends as indicated and work through both thicknesses at overlap areas to join), B, C and D pieces according to graphs. Using White/Gold, Straight Stitch and Backstitch, embroider detail as indicated on C#2 graph.

2: Follow Step 4 of Foyer & Kitchen Door Walls & Floor Stitching Instructions on page 82.

3: Whipstitch remaining vertical wall supports to B and D according to Door Wall Support Assembly Illustrations on this page and Exterior and Interior Wall Support Attachment Diagrams on pages 72 and 31. Fit notches together and tack horizontal supports to vertical supports (see Support Interlocking and Tacking Diagrams on page 20).

4: With White, Whipstitch C#1 door arch to B and C#2 arch to D. Positioning C#1/B door unit over floor as indicated, with colors to match floor, Whipstitch walls and supports to floor as indicated and according to Door Wall Assembly Diagram on page 83. Repeat with C#2/D door unit.

5: Placing assembled walls and floor over base, with indicated colors, follow Steps 1-4, 6 and 7 of Foyer/Kitchen Assembly Diagram on page 83.

Set aside.

WALL SUPPORT COLOR CODING KEY:

- B – Vertical Wall Support
- C – Vertical Wall Support
- D – Vertical Wall Support
- E – Vertical Wall Support
- F – Horizontal Wall Support
- H – Horizontal Wall Support
- I – Horizontal Wall Support
- J – Horizontal Wall Support
- K – Horizontal Wall Support
- L – Horizontal Wall Support

Door Wall Support Assembly Illustrations

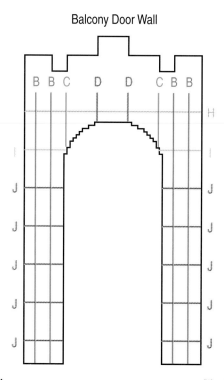

Balcony Door Wall

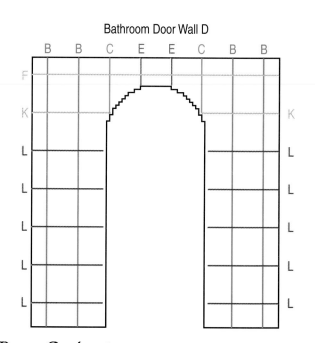

Bathroom Door Wall D

B – Balcony Door Wall (cut 1) 58 x 103 holes

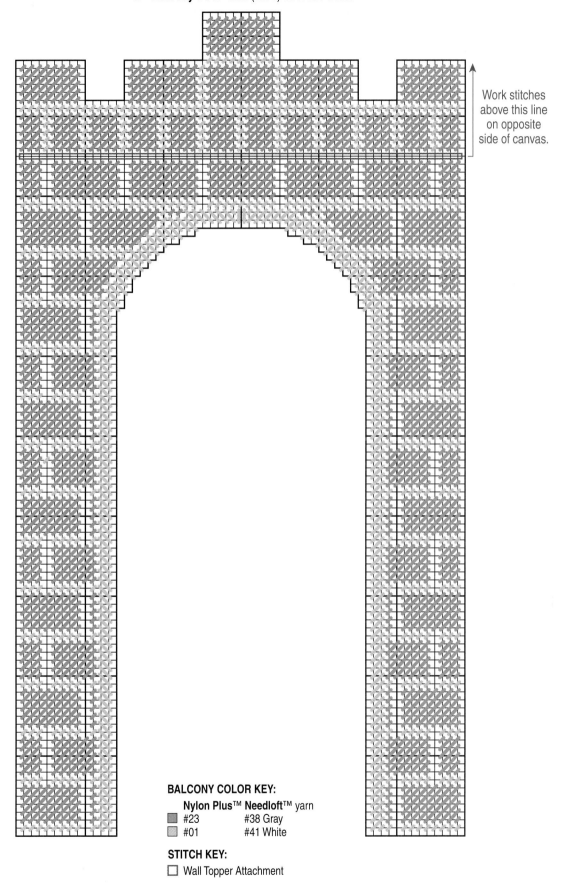

Work stitches above this line on opposite side of canvas.

BALCONY COLOR KEY:

Nylon Plus™ Needloft™ yarn

▨	#23		#38 Gray
▨	#01		#41 White

STITCH KEY:

□ Wall Topper Attachment

C – Upper Floor Foyer Door Wall #2
(cut 1) 80 x 85 holes

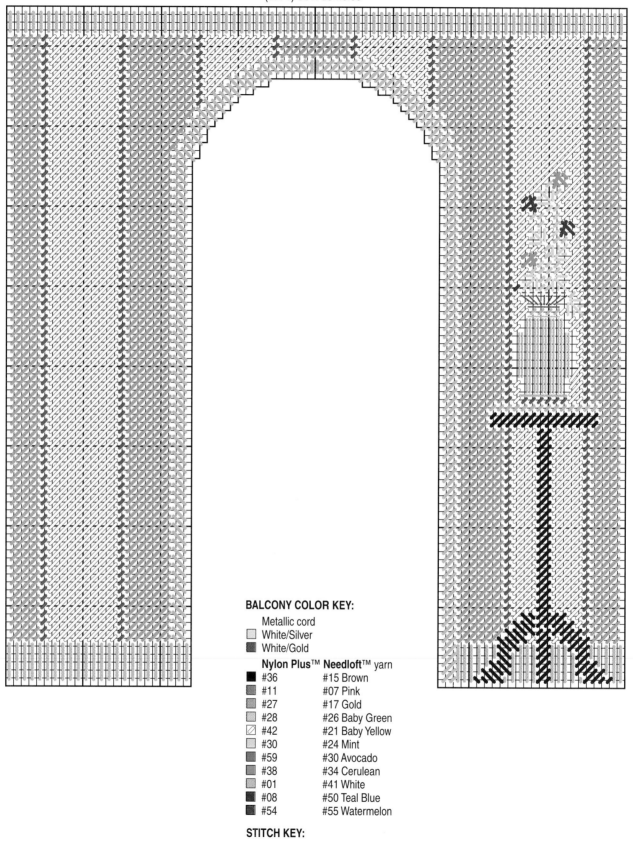

BALCONY COLOR KEY:

Metallic cord

☐ White/Silver
☐ White/Gold

Nylon Plus™ Needloft™ yarn

■ #36		#15 Brown
■ #11		#07 Pink
■ #27		#17 Gold
☐ #28		#26 Baby Green
◪ #42		#21 Baby Yellow
☐ #30		#24 Mint
■ #59		#30 Avocado
■ #38		#34 Cerulean
☐ #01		#41 White
■ #08		#50 Teal Blue
■ #54		#55 Watermelon

STITCH KEY:

— Backstitch/Straight Stitch

D – Bathroom Door Wall
(cut 1) 80 x 85 holes

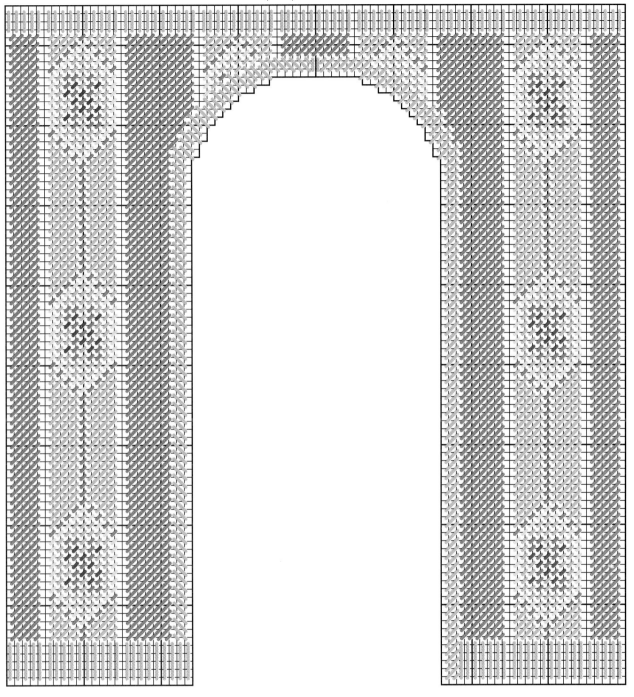

BALCONY EXTERIOR, DOORS & FINISHING

CUTTING INSTRUCTIONS:

NOTES: Graphs, illustration and diagrams on pages 108-113. Use stiff canvas throughout.

A: For balcony exterior front, cut one according to graph.

B: For balcony exterior left and right side walls, cut one each according to graphs.

C: For balcony trim front, cut one according to graph.

D: For balcony trim left and right sides, cut one each according to graph.

E: For balcony trim mortar pieces, cut two 1 x 12 holes (no graph).

F: For balcony wall topper, cut one according to graph.

G: For balcony door wall trim, cut one according to graph.

H: For balcony and bathroom door wall toppers, cut one 3 x 58 holes and one 3 x 80 holes.

I: For balcony double door sides #1 and #2, cut two each according to Double Door Side D graphs on page 94.

J: For bathroom double door sides #1 and #2, cut two each according to graphs.

K: For door hinges, cut four 3 x 34 holes (no graph).

L: For washers, cut two according to graph.

STITCHING INSTRUCTIONS:

NOTE: E and L pieces are unworked.

1: Using colors and stitches indicated, work A-D and F-J pieces according to graphs. (**NOTE:** If desired, Slanted Gobelin Stitch over 3 bars may be substituted for Special Sheaf Stitch on doors.) Using White and Slanted Gobelin Stitch over narrow width, work K pieces.

2: Assemble C-E pieces according to Balcony Trim Assembly Diagram.

3: With indicated colors, assemble A-H pieces as indicated and according to Balcony Exterior Assembly Diagram.

4: Attaching strung bead or berry bead handles to doors as in Step 1 of Entrance and Double Door Assembly Diagrams on page 95, assemble I-K pieces according to Double Door Assembly Diagram.

5: Attach closures to each castle section according to Closure Diagrams.

BALCONY & FINISHING COLOR KEY:
Nylon Plus™ Needloft™ yarn
- #23   #38 Gray
- #01   #41 White

STITCH KEY:
☐ Wall Topper Attachment

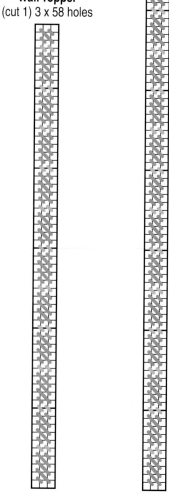

H – Bathroom Door Wall Topper
(cut 1) 3 x 80 holes

H – Balcony Door Wall Topper
(cut 1) 3 x 58 holes

A – Balcony Exterior Front
(cut 1) 48 x 80 holes

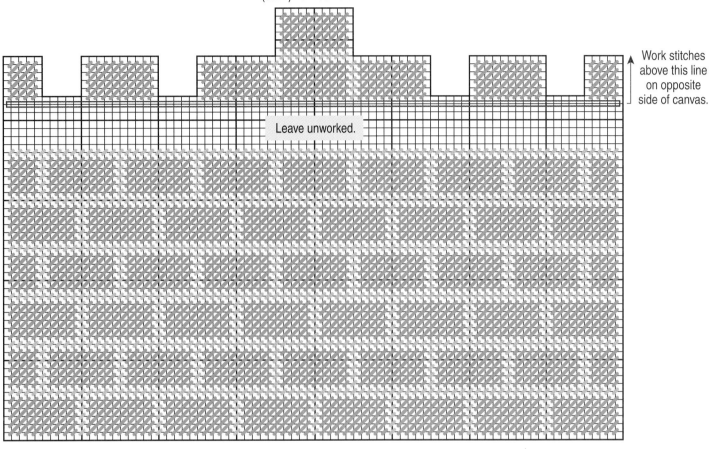

Leave unworked.

Work stitches above this line on opposite side of canvas.

B – Balcony Exterior Left Side Wall (cut 1) 35 x 42 holes

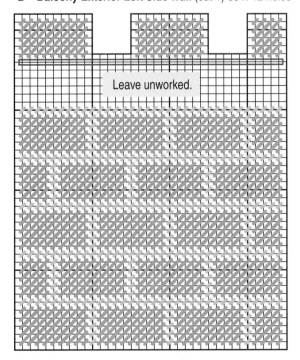

Leave unworked.

B – Balcony Exterior Right Side Wall (cut 1) 35 x 42 holes

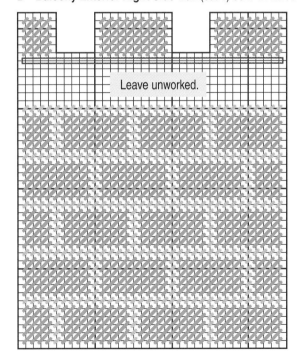

Leave unworked.

C – Balcony Trim Front (cut 1) 18 x 80 holes
G – Balcony Door Wall Trim (cut 1) 18 x 58 holes

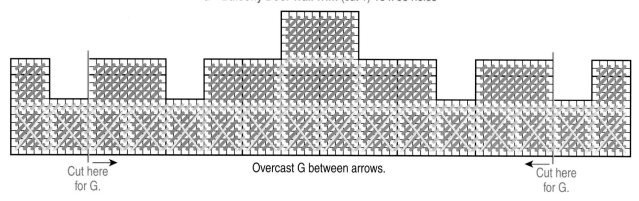

Cut here
for G.

Overcast G between arrows.

Cut here
for G.

D – Balcony Trim Left Side (cut 1) 12 x 35 holes

L – Washer
(cut 2) 6 x 6 holes

Cut Out

Overcast with
White/Silver.

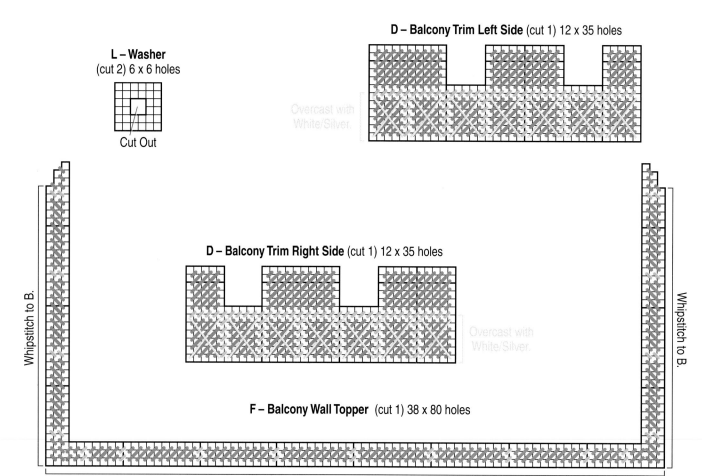

D – Balcony Trim Right Side (cut 1) 12 x 35 holes

Overcast with
White/Silver.

Whipstitch to B.

Whipstitch to B.

F – Balcony Wall Topper (cut 1) 38 x 80 holes

Whipstitch to A.

BALCONY & FINISHING COLOR KEY:

Metallic cord
☐ White/Silver
Nylon Plus™ Needloft™ yarn
■ #23   #38 Gray
☐ #01   #41 White

STITCH KEY:

— Backstitch/Straight Stitch

Balcony Trim Assembly Diagram

Step 1:
With matching colors, Whipstitch
C, D and E pieces together.

Step 2:
With White/Silver, Overcast side edges of D pieces (see
graphs) and bottom edges of assembled trim pieces.

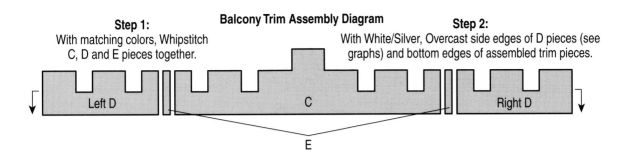

**J – Bathroom Double
Door Side #1**
(cut 2) 14 x 74 holes

**J – Bathroom Double
Door Side #2**
(cut 2) 14 x 74 holes

Do not Whipstitch; attach to K.

Do not Whipstitch; attach to K.

NOTE: Work crossed stitch areas
according to Special Sheaf Stitch Illustration.

Special Sheaf Stitch Illustration

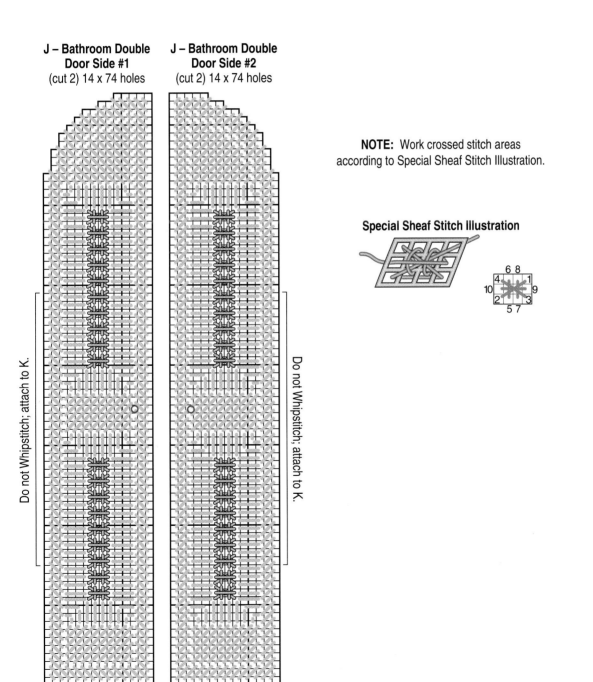

**Balcony Exterior
Assembly Diagram**

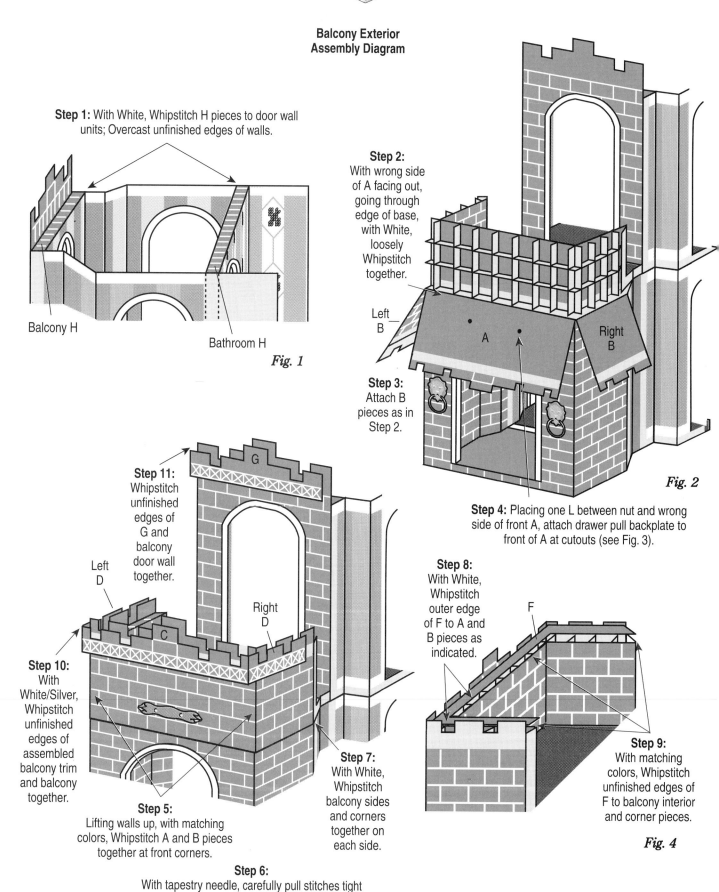

Step 1: With White, Whipstitch H pieces to door wall units; Overcast unfinished edges of walls.

Balcony H

Bathroom H

Fig. 1

Step 2: With wrong side of A facing out, going through edge of base, with White, loosely Whipstitch together.

Left B

Right B

A

Step 3: Attach B pieces as in Step 2.

Fig. 2

Step 4: Placing one L between nut and wrong side of front A, attach drawer pull backplate to front of A at cutouts (see Fig. 3).

Step 11: Whipstitch unfinished edges of G and balcony door wall together.

G

Left D

C

Right D

Step 10: With White/Silver, Whipstitch unfinished edges of assembled balcony trim and balcony together.

Step 5: Lifting walls up, with matching colors, Whipstitch A and B pieces together at front corners.

Step 6: With tapestry needle, carefully pull stitches tight at bottom edge of walls.

Step 7: With White, Whipstitch balcony sides and corners together on each side.

Fig. 3

Step 8: With White, Whipstitch outer edge of F to A and B pieces as indicated.

F

Step 9: With matching colors, Whipstitch unfinished edges of F to balcony interior and corner pieces.

Fig. 4

Closure Diagrams

Step 1:
Cutting sizes indicated, sew or glue fuzzy sides of closure pieces to door walls, wall ends, and turret sides of Dining Room/Bedroom section as shown; repeat on Living Room/Study section.

CLOSURE COLOR CODING KEY:
- 3/4" pieces
- 1/2" pieces

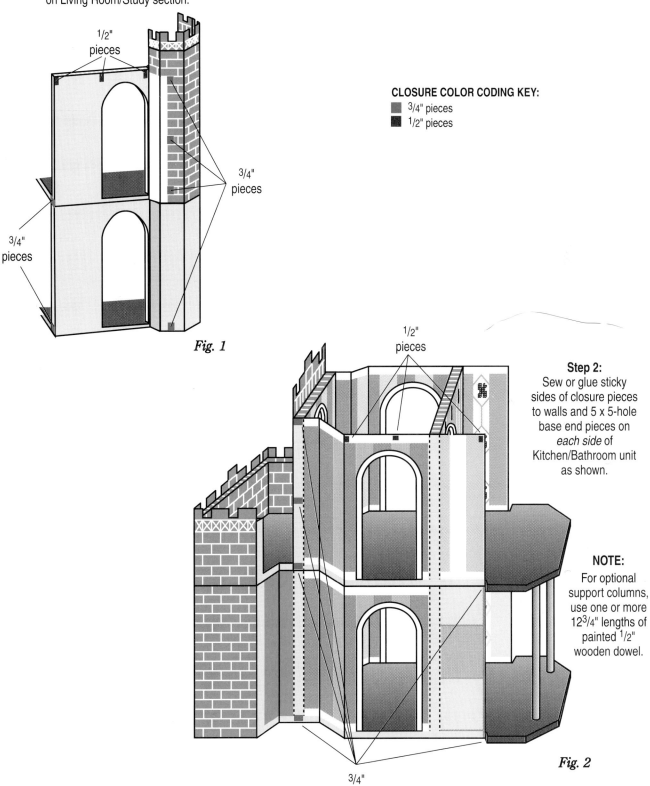

1/2" pieces

3/4" pieces

3/4" pieces

Fig. 1

1/2" pieces

Step 2:
Sew or glue sticky sides of closure pieces to walls and 5 x 5-hole base end pieces on *each side* of Kitchen/Bathroom unit as shown.

NOTE:
For optional support columns, use one or more 12³/₄" lengths of painted ¹/₂" wooden dowel.

3/4" pieces

Fig. 2

Dream Furnishings

Real-life detail and historical charm create elegant furnishings and decorating accessories for each room.

Living Room

NOTE: For materials for all furnishings, see page 145.

SIZE: Sofa is 3¾" x 8" x about 6¼" tall; Chair is 3¾" x 4½" x 6¼" tall; Tall Table is 3¼" across x 4¾" tall; Short Table is 4½" across x 3¼" tall; Fireplace Grate is 2" x 2½" x ¾" tall; Fireplace Screen is 1" x 3⅞" x 3⅞" tall.

MATERIALS:
☐ Five sheets of stiff 12" x 18" 7-count plastic canvas
☐ ½ sheet of standard-size flexible 7-count plastic canvas (use for pillow pieces)
☐ ½ sheet of black 7-count plastic canvas
☐ One 3" and one 4¼" Crafty Circle
☐ Three 2½"-long ⅝" wooden dowels or tree branches
☐ Brown acrylic paint (optional)
☐ Two large scalloped lace motifs
☐ Polyester fiberfill
☐ Craft glue or glue gun
☐ Metallic cord; for amounts see Color Key on page 118.
☐ Worsted-weight or plastic canvas yarn; for amounts see Color Key.

NOTE: Graphs and diagrams on pages 118-121.

SOFA

CUTTING INSTRUCTIONS:

NOTE: Use clear canvas throughout.

A: For back and back lining, cut one each according to graphs.

B: For front, cut one according to graph.

C: For cushion support, cut one 23 x 47 holes.

D: For inner and outer ends, cut two each according to graphs.

E: For armrests, cut two 2 x 39 holes.

F: For bottom, cut one 23 x 52 holes.

G: For leg pieces, cut ten according to graph.

H: For cushion front, cut one 21 x 45 holes.

I: For cushion back, cut one 24 x 45 holes (no graph).

J: For cushion seat, cut one 19 x 45 holes.

K: For cushion bottom, cut one 22 x 45 holes (no graph).

L: For cushion sides, cut two according to graph.

M: For cushion top and front edges, cut one each 3 x 45 holes.

N: For pillow sides, cut two 16 x 19 holes.

O: For pillow ends, cut four according to graph.

STITCHING INSTRUCTIONS:

NOTE: Six G, I and K pieces are unworked.

1: Using colors and stitches indicated, work A-F (one of each D on opposite side of canvas), four G (two on opposite side of canvas), H, J, L, M, N (overlap three holes as indicated on graph and work through both thicknesses at overlap area to join) and O pieces according to graphs. With Brown, Overcast unfinished bottom edge of Sofa Back A and top edge of each worked G as indicated.

2: Using Brown and French Knot, embroider buttons on pillow ends as indicated.

NOTE: Stuff assembled pieces with fiberfill before closing.

3: With matching colors (see photo), Whipstitch A-F pieces together according to Sofa/Chair Assembly Diagram.

4: To finish each leg, with Brown, Whipstitch pieces together according to Sofa/Chair Leg Assembly Diagrams; glue tops of legs to worked areas of Sofa bottom.

5: For cushion, with Mint, Whipstitch H-M pieces together as indicated and according to Sofa/Chair Cushion Assembly Diagram. Glue one lace motif to cushion back as shown in photo.

6: For each pillow, with Brown, Whipstitch one N and two O pieces together according to Pillow Assembly Diagram.

CHAIR

CUTTING INSTRUCTIONS:

NOTE: Use clear canvas throughout.

A: For back and back lining, cut one each according to graphs.

B: For front, cut one according to graph.

C: For cushion support, cut one 23 x 23 holes.

D: For inner and outer ends, cut two each according to graph.

E: For armrests, cut two 2 x 39 holes.

F: For bottom, cut one 23 x 28 holes.

G: For leg pieces, cut ten according to graph.

H: For cushion front, cut one 21 x 21 holes.

I: For cushion back, cut one 21 x 24 holes (no graph).

J: For cushion seat, cut one 19 x 21 holes.

K: For cushion bottom, cut one 21 x 22 holes (no graph).

L: For cushion sides, cut two according to graph.

M: For cushion top and front edges, cut one each 3 x 21 holes.

STITCHING INSTRUCTIONS:

1: Using Chair pieces in place of Sofa pieces, follow Stitching Instructions for Sofa on this page.

TABLES

CUTTING INSTRUCTIONS:

NOTE: Use clear canvas throughout.

A: For Tall Tabletop, use 3" Crafty Circle (no graph).

B: For Tall Tabletop lip, cut one 2 x 68 holes (no graph).

C: For Tall Table center leg pieces, cut three according to graph.

D: For Tall Table side leg pieces, cut six according to graph.

E: For Short Tabletop, use 4¼" Crafty Circle (no graph).

F: For Short Tabletop lip, cut one 2 x 90 holes (no graph).

G: For Short Table center leg pieces, cut three according to graph.

H: For Short Table side leg pieces, cut six according to graph.

STITCHING INSTRUCTIONS:

NOTES: Use Continental Stitch throughout. One C, two D, one G and two H pieces are unworked.

1: Using White, work A and E pieces. Using Brown, work two C, four D (two on opposite side of canvas), two G and four H (two on opposite side of canvas) pieces according to graphs; work B (overlap four holes at ends and work through both thicknesses at overlap area to join) and F (Whipstitch ends together) pieces.

2: For Tall Table, with Brown, Whipstitch C and D pieces together as indicated and according to Table Leg Assembly Diagram. With White, Whipstitch A and B pieces together; with Brown, Overcast unfinished edges. Glue tabletop and leg assembly together.

3: For Short Table, using E-H pieces in place of A-D pieces, follow Steps 1 and 2.

NOTE: Cut gold metallic cord into two 9" lengths.

4: Glue one length of cord around inner edge of each tabletop between Continental and Whipstitches.

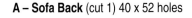

FIREPLACE GRATE & SCREEN

CUTTING INSTRUCTIONS:

NOTE: Use black canvas for A-E pieces and clear canvas for F pieces.

A: For grate top, cut one according to graph.

B: For grate base sides, cut two according to graph.

C: For grate base ends, cut two according to graph.

D: For screen front, cut one according to graph.

E: For screen braces, cut two according to graph.

F: For screen ornaments, cut two according to graph.

STITCHING INSTRUCTIONS:

NOTES: A-E pieces are un-worked. If desired, paint dowels or branches brown.

1: Using metallic cord and stitches indicated, work F pieces according to graph; Overcast unfinished edges.

2: With Black, Whipstitch A-C pieces together as indicated and according to Grate Assembly Diagram. Whipstitch D and E pieces together as indicated and according to Screen Assembly Diagram. Glue logs together and to grate, and ornaments to screen front as shown in photo on page 56.

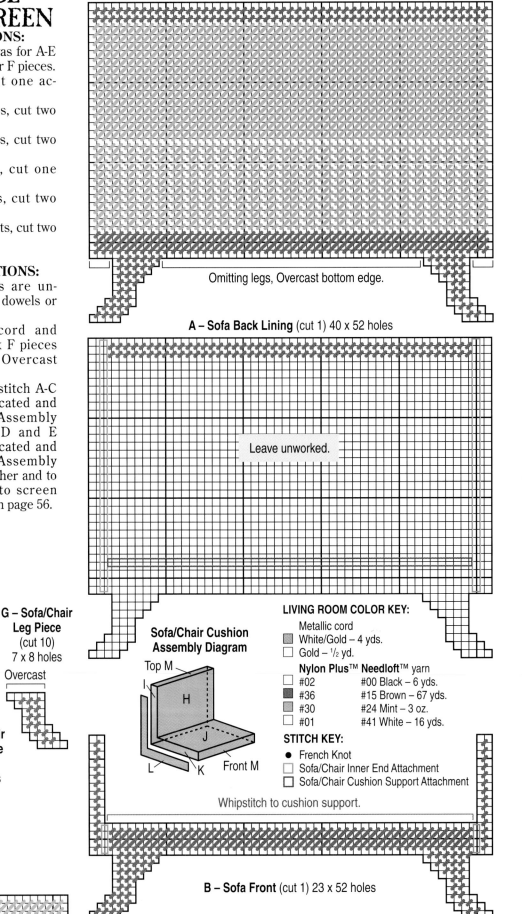

A – Sofa Back (cut 1) 40 x 52 holes

Omitting legs, Overcast bottom edge.

A – Sofa Back Lining (cut 1) 40 x 52 holes

Leave unworked.

E – Sofa/Chair Armrest (cut 2) 2 x 39 holes

G – Sofa/Chair Leg Piece (cut 10) 7 x 8 holes

Overcast

L – Sofa/Chair Cushion Side (cut 2) 22 x 24 holes

Sofa/Chair Cushion Assembly Diagram

Top M
I
H
J
L
K
Front M

Whipstitch to cushion support.

B – Sofa Front (cut 1) 23 x 52 holes

LIVING ROOM COLOR KEY:

Metallic cord
- ▨ White/Gold – 4 yds.
- ☐ Gold – ½ yd.

Nylon Plus™ Needloft™ yarn
- ☐ #02   #00 Black – 6 yds.
- ■ #36   #15 Brown – 67 yds.
- ▨ #30   #24 Mint – 3 oz.
- ☐ #01   #41 White – 16 yds.

STITCH KEY:
- ● French Knot
- ☐ Sofa/Chair Inner End Attachment
- ☐ Sofa/Chair Cushion Support Attachment

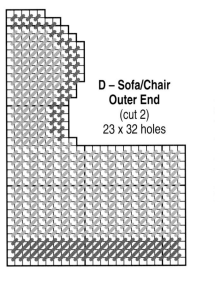

**D – Sofa/Chair
Outer End**
(cut 2)
23 x 32 holes

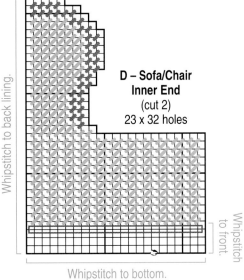

**D – Sofa/Chair
Inner End**
(cut 2)
23 x 32 holes

Whipstitch to back lining.

Whipstitch to bottom.

Whipstitch to front.

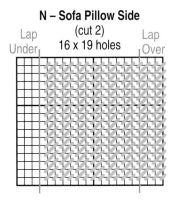

N – Sofa Pillow Side
(cut 2)
16 x 19 holes

Lap Under

Lap Over

Sofa/Chair Assembly Diagram

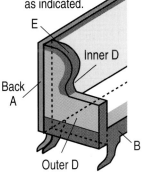

Step 1:
Whipstitch back lining
A, C, inner D pieces
and F together as
indicated.

Step 2:
Whipstitch assembly
and remaining A, B, D
and E pieces together
as indicated.

Back lining A

Inner D

C

F

E

Inner D

Back A

Outer D

B

O – Sofa Pillow End
(cut 4)
5 x 5 holes

**Pillow
Assembly Diagram**

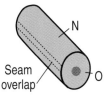

N

Seam
overlap

O

J – Sofa Cushion Seat (cut 1) 19 x 45 holes

Whipstitch to H.

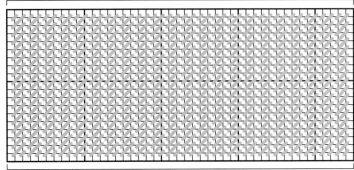

Whipstitch to front M.

**Sofa/Chair Leg
Assembly Diagrams**

Front Leg

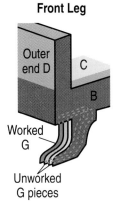

Outer
end D

C

B

Worked
G

Unworked
G pieces

Back Leg

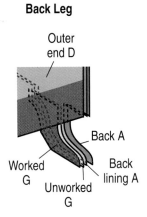

Outer
end D

Back A

Back
lining A

Worked
G

Unworked
G

H – Sofa Cushion Front (cut 1) 21 x 45 holes

Whipstitch to top M.

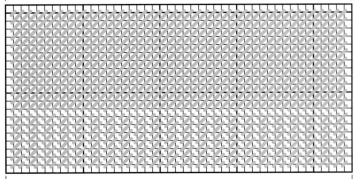

Whipstitch to J.

M – Sofa Cushion Top & Front Edge
(cut 1 each) 3 x 45 holes

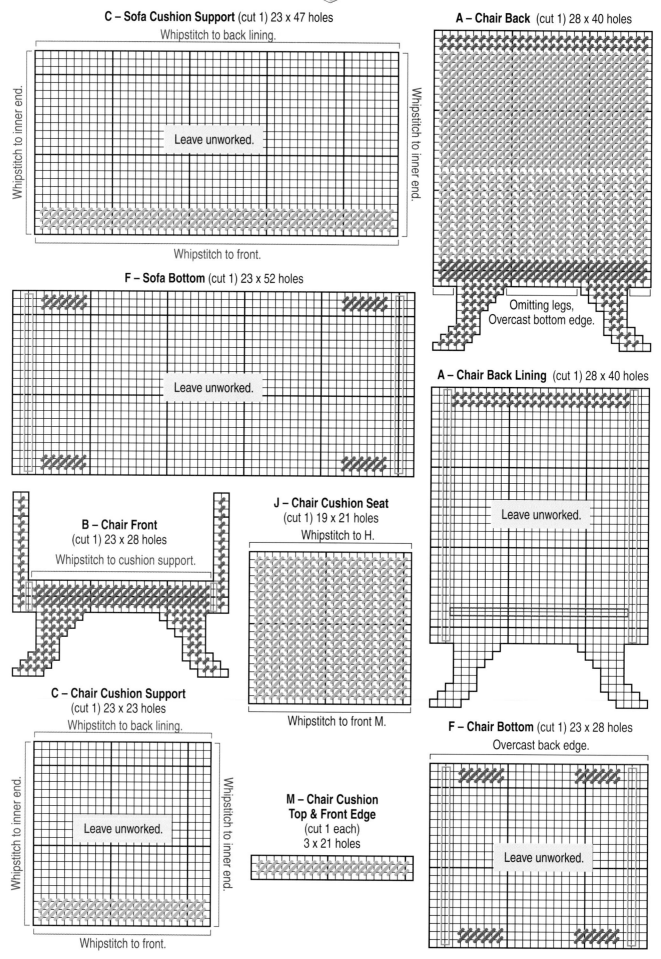

C – Sofa Cushion Support (cut 1) 23 x 47 holes

Whipstitch to back lining.

Whipstitch to inner end.

Whipstitch to inner end.

Leave unworked.

Whipstitch to front.

F – Sofa Bottom (cut 1) 23 x 52 holes

Leave unworked.

B – Chair Front
(cut 1) 23 x 28 holes

Whipstitch to cushion support.

C – Chair Cushion Support
(cut 1) 23 x 23 holes

Whipstitch to back lining.

Whipstitch to inner end.

Whipstitch to inner end.

Leave unworked.

Whipstitch to front.

J – Chair Cushion Seat
(cut 1) 19 x 21 holes

Whipstitch to H.

Whipstitch to front M.

**M – Chair Cushion
Top & Front Edge**
(cut 1 each)
3 x 21 holes

A – Chair Back (cut 1) 28 x 40 holes

Omitting legs,
Overcast bottom edge.

A – Chair Back Lining (cut 1) 28 x 40 holes

Leave unworked.

F – Chair Bottom (cut 1) 23 x 28 holes

Overcast back edge.

Leave unworked.

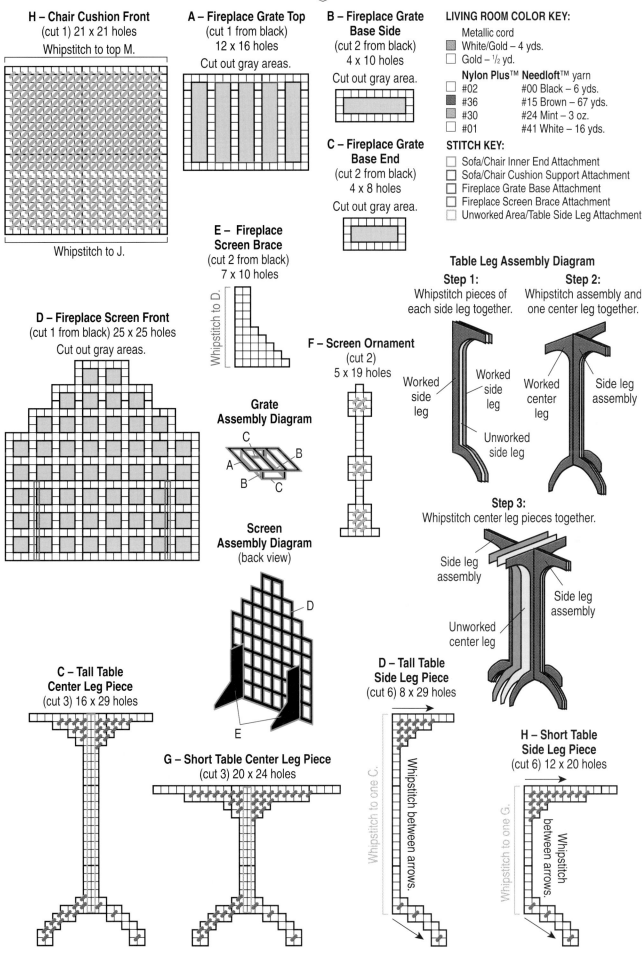

H – Chair Cushion Front
(cut 1) 21 x 21 holes
Whipstitch to top M.
Whipstitch to J.

A – Fireplace Grate Top
(cut 1 from black)
12 x 16 holes
Cut out gray areas.

B – Fireplace Grate Base Side
(cut 2 from black)
4 x 10 holes
Cut out gray area.

C – Fireplace Grate Base End
(cut 2 from black)
4 x 8 holes
Cut out gray area.

LIVING ROOM COLOR KEY:
Metallic cord
White/Gold – 4 yds.
Gold – ½ yd.

Nylon Plus™ Needloft™ yarn
#02   #00 Black – 6 yds.
#36   #15 Brown – 67 yds.
#30   #24 Mint – 3 oz.
#01   #41 White – 16 yds.

STITCH KEY:
Sofa/Chair Inner End Attachment
Sofa/Chair Cushion Support Attachment
Fireplace Grate Base Attachment
Fireplace Screen Brace Attachment
Unworked Area/Table Side Leg Attachment

E – Fireplace Screen Brace
(cut 2 from black)
7 x 10 holes
Whipstitch to D.

D – Fireplace Screen Front
(cut 1 from black) 25 x 25 holes
Cut out gray areas.

F – Screen Ornament
(cut 2)
5 x 19 holes

Grate Assembly Diagram
C
A   B
B   C

Screen Assembly Diagram
(back view)
D
E

Table Leg Assembly Diagram

Step 1:
Whipstitch pieces of each side leg together.
Worked side leg
Worked side leg
Unworked side leg

Step 2:
Whipstitch assembly and one center leg together.
Worked center leg
Side leg assembly

Step 3:
Whipstitch center leg pieces together.
Side leg assembly
Side leg assembly
Unworked center leg

C – Tall Table Center Leg Piece
(cut 3) 16 x 29 holes

G – Short Table Center Leg Piece
(cut 3) 20 x 24 holes

D – Tall Table Side Leg Piece
(cut 6) 8 x 29 holes
Whipstitch to one C.
Whipstitch between arrows.

H – Short Table Side Leg Piece
(cut 6) 12 x 20 holes
Whipstitch to one G.
Whipstitch between arrows.

Study

SIZE: Desk is 4½" x 8⅝" x 4⅜" tall; Chair is 2¾" x 3½" x 7⅜" tall; Table is 2" x 3¾" x 4½" tall; Bookcase is 1½" x 3½" x 5⅛" tall; each Small Book is 1" x 1¼"; each Large Book is 1¼" x 1¾"; Lamp is 4⅛" tall; Inkwell is ¾" square x about 3" tall; Fireplace Grate is 2" x 2½" x ¾" tall; Fireplace Screen is 1" x 3⅞" x 3⅞" tall.

MATERIALS:
- ☐ Two sheets of stiff 12" x 18" 7-count plastic canvas
- ☐ One sheet of black 7-count plastic canvas
- ☐ One sheet of ivory 7-count plastic canvas
- ☐ ½ sheet of brown 7-count plastic canvas
- ☐ Scraps of white 7-count plastic canvas
- ☐ Scraps of colored 7-count plastic canvas
- ☐ One white feather
- ☐ Two 6-mm. and four 3-mm. gold beads
- ☐ 36 clear and nine amber 4-mm. faceted beads
- ☐ 20⅝" clear 4-mm. prestrung pearls
- ☐ ½" tan ¾"-wide Velcro® closure
- ☐ Three 2½"-long ⅝" wooden dowels or tree branches
- ☐ Brown acrylic paint (optional)
- ☐ Sewing needle and matching color thread (thread optional)
- ☐ Craft glue or glue gun
- ☐ Embroidery floss; for amount see Color Key on page 125.
- ☐ Metallic cord; for amount see Color Key.
- ☐ Worsted-weight or plastic canvas yarn; for amounts see Color Key.

NOTE: Graphs, illustrations and diagrams on pages 124-127.

DESK
CUTTING INSTRUCTIONS:
NOTE: Use clear canvas for A-H pieces and white canvas for I pieces.
A: For front and back, cut one each according to graphs.
B: For inner and outer ends, cut two each 23 x 28 holes.
C: For cabinet bottoms, cut two 13 x 23 holes (no graph).
D: For top, cut one 29 x 56 holes.
E: For blotter, cut one 23 x 50 holes.
F: For small drawer facades, cut two 3 x 11 holes.
G: For large drawer facade, cut one 3 x 22 holes.

H: For doors, cut two 11 x 17 holes.
I: For knob backs, cut five according to graph.

STITCHING INSTRUCTIONS:
NOTE: C and I pieces are unworked.
1: With Camel, Overcast unfinished edges of F and G pieces. Using colors and stitches indicated, work A, B, D, E, F, G (hold F and G pieces to Desk Front A as indicated on graph and work through both thicknesses as one) and H pieces according to graphs; Overcast unfinished cutout edges of Desk Front A and unfinished edges of D and E pieces.
2: With matching colors, sew and Whipstitch pieces together according to Desk Assembly Diagram; Overcast unfinished edges.
NOTE: Cut closure into two ¼" pieces.
3: Sew or glue closures to inside of doors and corresponding areas on front.

CHAIR
CUTTING INSTRUCTIONS:
NOTE: Use clear canvas for A-D pieces.
A: For back pieces, cut one each according to graphs.
B: For front legs, cut one according to graph.
C: For side legs, cut two according to graph.
D: For seat, cut one according to graph.

STITCHING INSTRUCTIONS:
1: Using colors and stitches indicated, work A-D pieces according to graphs; Overcast unfinished cutout edges of A#2-C pieces.
2: With Camel, Whipstitch pieces together according to Chair Assembly Diagram; Overcast unfinished edges.

TABLE
CUTTING INSTRUCTIONS:
NOTE: Use clear canvas throughout.
A: For top, cut one according to graph.
B: For top lip front and back, cut one 2 x 40 holes and one 2 x 24 holes (no graphs).
C: For front legs, cut two according to graph.
D: For back legs, cut one according to graph.

STITCHING INSTRUCTIONS:
1: Using colors and stitches indicated, work A, C and D pieces according to graphs. Using Camel and Continental Stitch, work B pieces.
2: To assemble legs and top, with Camel, Whipstitch pieces together according to Table Assembly Diagram; Overcast unfinished edges. Glue top to leg assembly.

BOOKCASE
CUTTING INSTRUCTIONS:
NOTE: Use brown canvas for one A and clear canvas for remaining pieces.
A: For back pieces, cut one from brown and one from clear according to graph.
B: For inner and outer side pieces, cut two each according to graphs.
C: For shelves, cut two 9 x 20 holes (no graph).

STITCHING INSTRUCTIONS:
NOTE: Brown A is unworked.
1: Using colors and stitches indicated, work A and B (one each on opposite side of canvas) pieces according to graphs. Using Camel and Slanted Gobelin Stitch over narrow width, work C pieces.
2: With Camel, Whipstitch pieces together according to Bookcase Assembly Diagram; Whipstitch and Overcast unfinished edges.

LAMP & INKWELL
CUTTING INSTRUCTIONS:
NOTE: Use clear canvas throughout.
A: For Lamp shade, cut one according to graph.
B: For Lamp shade top and pole top, cut one each according to graph.
C: For Lamp pole sides, cut four according to graph.
D: For Lamp bottom, cut one 7 x 7 holes (no graph).
E: For Inkwell base pieces, cut two 5 x 5 holes.
F: For Inkwell pieces, cut three 3 x 3 holes (no graph).

STITCHING INSTRUCTIONS:
NOTES: B, D, E and two F pieces are unworked. Cut one 6" and nine 1⅝" lengths of prestrung pearls.
1: For Lamp shade, with six strands floss, assemble pearls, beads, A and one B according to Bead Strand Illustration and Shade

Assembly Diagram.

2: For Lamp pole, using metallic cord and stitches indicated, work C pieces according to graph; assemble remaining B, C and D pieces according to Pole Assembly Diagram.

3: For Inkwell , using cord and Continental Stitch, work one F; Whipstitch E and F pieces together as indicated and according to Inkwell Assembly Diagram. Insert feather in top for quill pen.

BOOKS

CUTTING INSTRUCTIONS:

A: For Large Book covers, cut sixteen from black 8 x 11 holes (no graph).

B: For Large Book pages, cut thirty-two from ivory 8 x 11 holes (no graph).

C: For Small Book covers, cut sixteen (two from each color to make eight books) 6 x 8 holes (no graph).

D: For Small Book pages, cut thirty-two from ivory 6 x 8 holes (no graph).

STITCHING INSTRUCTIONS:

NOTE: Pieces are unworked.

1: For each Large Book, with Black, Whipstitch two A and four B

Special Sheaf Stitch Illustration

B – Desk Inner & Outer End
(cut 2 each)
23 x 28 holes

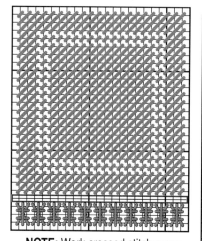

NOTE: Work crossed stitch areas according to Special Sheaf Stitch Illustration.

pieces together according to Book Assembly Diagram.

2: For each Small Book, using C and D pieces in place of A and B pieces and with yarn scraps, follow Step 1.

FIREPLACE GRATE & SCREEN

Follow instructions for Living Room Fireplace Grate & Screen on page 118.

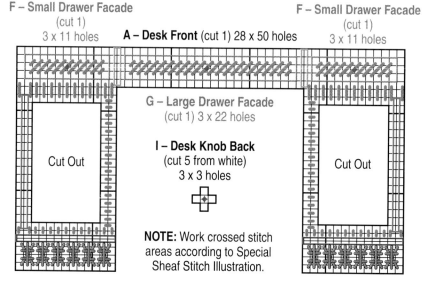

A – Desk Back (cut 1) 28 x 50 holes

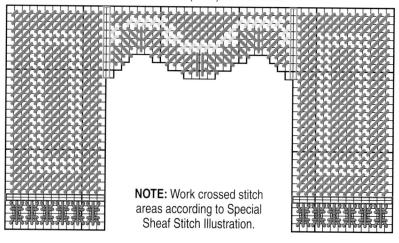

NOTE: Work crossed stitch areas according to Special Sheaf Stitch Illustration.

D – Desktop (cut 1) 29 x 56 holes

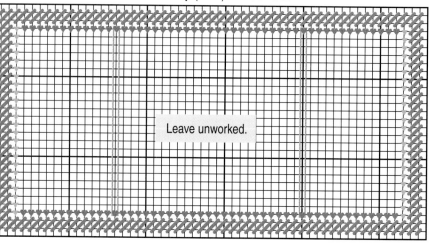

Leave unworked.

STUDY COLOR KEY:

Embroidery floss
☐ White – 3 yds.

Metallic cord
☐ White/Gold – 15 yds.

Nylon Plus™ Needloft™ yarn
☐ #02	#00 Black – 6 yds.	
■ #38	#34 Cerulean – 2 yds.	
☐ #01	#41 White – 12 yds.	
☐ #34	#43 Camel – 3½ oz.	
☐ #08	#50 Teal Blue – 2 yds.	

STITCH KEY:

✦ Desk Knob Attachment
☐ Desk Door Attachment
☐ Unworked Area/Desk Cabinet Bottom Attachment
▽ Desk Outer Side Attachment
☐ Unworked Area/Desk Inner Side Attachment
♥ Desk Front & Back Attachment
☐ Unworked Area/Bookcase Shelf Attachment

E – Desk Blotter (cut 1) 23 x 50 holes

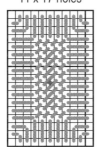

H – Desk Door
(cut 2)
11 x 17 holes

D – Table Back Legs
(cut 1)
20 x 28 holes

C – Table Front Legs
(cut 2)
13 x 28 holes

A – Tabletop (cut 1) 13 x 24 holes

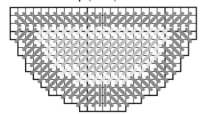

Table Assembly Diagram
Step 1:
Whipstitch A and B pieces together.

Back B
A

Step 2:
Whipstitch C
and D pieces
together.

D
Front B

C   C

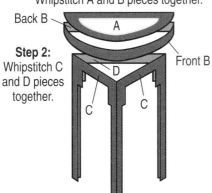

A – Bookcase Back Piece
(cut 1 from each color)
20 x 34 holes

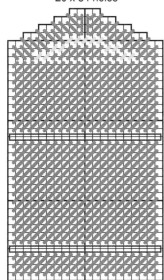

Bookcase Assembly Diagram

Step 1:
Whipstitch worked A, inner side B
and C pieces together as indicated.

Step 2:
Whipstitch assembly, outer sides
and unworked A together.

Worked
A

Inner
side B

Inner
side B

C

Unworked
A

Outer
side B

Outer
side B

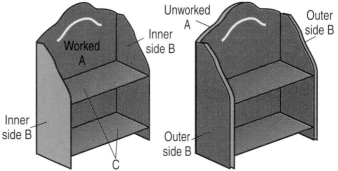
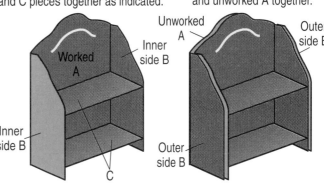

B – Bookcase Outer Side
(cut 2)
9 x 30 holes

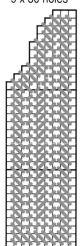

B – Bookcase Inner Side
(cut 2)
9 x 30 holes

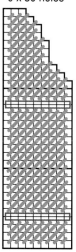

A – Chair Back #2
(cut 1)
18 x 48 holes

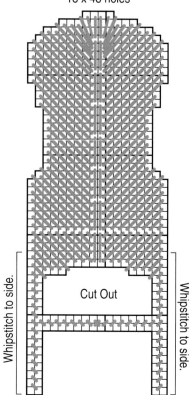

Whipstitch to side.

Cut Out

Whipstitch to side.

A – Chair Back #1
(cut 1)
18 x 30 holes

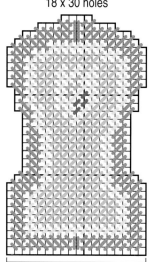

Whipstitch to D.

STUDY COLOR KEY:

Embroidery floss
☐ White – 3 yds.

Metallic cord
☐ White/Gold – 15 yds.

Nylon Plus™ Needloft™ yarn
☐ #02   #00 Black – 6 yds.
■ #38   #34 Cerulean – 2 yds.
☐ #01   #41 White – 12 yds.
■ #34   #43 Camel – 3 1/2 oz.
■ #08   #50 Teal Blue – 2 yds.

STITCH KEY:
☐ Unworked Area/Bookcase Shelf Attachment
☐ Inkwell Attachment

B – Chair Front Legs
(cut 1) 18 x 22 holes

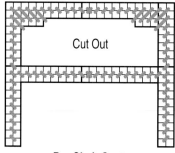

Cut Out

C – Chair Side Legs
(cut 2)
16 x 18 holes

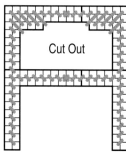

Cut Out

D – Chair Seat
(cut 1)
16 x 22 holes

Whipstitch to Back A#1.

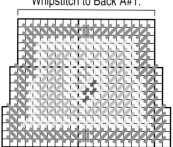

Chair Assembly Diagram

Step 1:
Whipstitch A#1 and D
together as indicated.

Step 2:
Whipstitch assembly, A#2,
B and C pieces together.

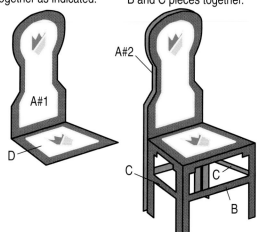

A#1

D

A#2

C   C

B

Bead Strand Illustration

Knotting one end, thread all faceted beads on several strands of floss in the order shown.

Clear bead

Amber bead

Shade Assembly Diagram

Step 4:
Sew bead to one B; glue B to top of shade.

3-mm. bead

Shade top B

Step 2:
Sew top three holes on extensions together as indicated.

Step 3:
Sew one 1⅝" length of pearls to each extension.

A

Overlap

Step 5:
Sew bead strand to bottom of shade.

Step 1:
Overlapping three holes and working through both thicknesses at overlap area to join ends as you work, sew 6" prestrung pearls to bottom of shade.

Pole Assembly Diagram

Pole top B

Step 2:
Glue remaining B to top of pole and inside of shade.

Step 1:
Whipstitch C and D pieces together.

C C

D

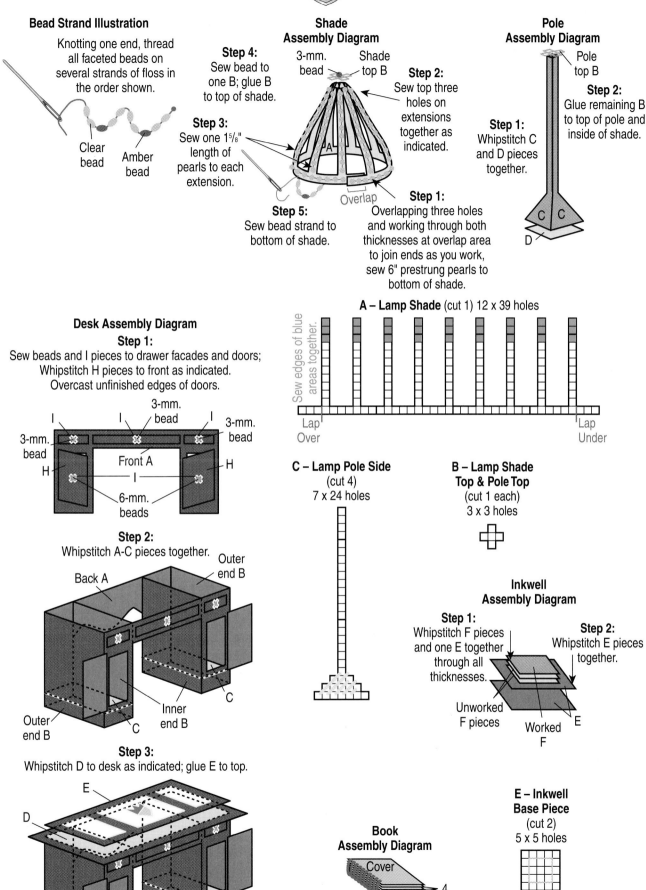

Desk Assembly Diagram
Step 1:
Sew beads and I pieces to drawer facades and doors; Whipstitch H pieces to front as indicated. Overcast unfinished edges of doors.

I   I   I

3-mm. bead

3-mm. bead

3-mm. bead

H   Front A   H

I

6-mm. beads

Step 2:
Whipstitch A-C pieces together.

Back A

Outer end B

Outer end B

Inner end B

C

C

Step 3:
Whipstitch D to desk as indicated; glue E to top.

E

D

A – Lamp Shade (cut 1) 12 x 39 holes

Sew edges of blue areas together.

Lap Over

Lap Under

C – Lamp Pole Side
(cut 4)
7 x 24 holes

B – Lamp Shade Top & Pole Top
(cut 1 each)
3 x 3 holes

Inkwell Assembly Diagram

Step 1:
Whipstitch F pieces and one E together through all thicknesses.

Step 2:
Whipstitch E pieces together.

Unworked F pieces

Worked F

E

E – Inkwell Base Piece
(cut 2)
5 x 5 holes

Book Assembly Diagram

Cover

4 pages

Whipstitch through all thicknesses for spine.

Cover

ining Room

SIZE: Dining Table is 5¾" x 9⅛" x 4⅝" tall; each Chair is 2¾" x 3½" x 7⅜" tall; Table is 2" x 3¾" x 4½" tall; Vase is 1¼" square x 1⅛" tall; Round Doily is 2⅝" across; Half-Round Doily is 1⅜" x 2⅝"; Fireplace Grate is 2" x 2½" x ¾" tall; Fireplace Screen is 1" x 3⅞" x 3⅞" tall.

MATERIALS:
- ☐ Three sheets of stiff 12" x 18" 7-count plastic canvas
- ☐ ½ sheet of black 7-count plastic canvas
- ☐ Scraps of white 7-count plastic canvas
- ☐ Four 4" wooden ⅛" dowels or bamboo skewers
- ☐ Two white 15-mm. aurora borealis berry beads
- ☐ Two round toothpicks
- ☐ Blue crayon
- ☐ Three 2½"-long ⅝" wooden dowels or tree branches
- ☐ Brown acrylic paint (optional)
- ☐ Coordinating color ribbon rose bouquet
- ☐ Craft glue or glue gun
- ☐ Metallic cord; for amount see Color Key.
- ☐ Worsted-weight or plastic canvas yarn; for amounts see Color Key.

NOTE: Graphs and diagrams on pages 129-131.

DINING TABLE

CUTTING INSTRUCTIONS:

NOTE: Use clear canvas throughout.

A: For top pieces, cut one each according to graphs.

B: For top lip pieces, cut two 2 x 81 holes (no graph).

C: For side legs, cut two according to graph.

D: For end legs, cut two according to graph.

E: For inner leg pieces, cut four 3 x 28 holes (no graph).

F: For top base, cut one 29 x 36 holes (no graph).

STITCHING INSTRUCTIONS:

NOTE: F piece is unworked.

1: With Brown, Overcast unfinished edges of A#2; using stitches indicated, work A#1, A#2 (hold to A#1 as indicated on graph and work through both thicknesses as one), C and D pieces according to graphs. Using Continental Stitch, overlapping two holes at ends and working

through both thicknesses at overlap areas to join, work B pieces. Using Slanted Gobelin Stitch over narrow width, work E pieces.

2: Assemble pieces according to Dining Table Assembly Diagram.

CHAIRS

CUTTING INSTRUCTIONS:

NOTE: Use clear canvas throughout.

A: For back pieces, cut four each according to graphs.

B: For front legs, cut four according to graph.

C: For side legs, cut eight according to graph.

D: For seats, cut four according to graph.

STITCHING INSTRUCTIONS:

1: Using colors and stitches indicated, work A-D pieces according to graphs. With Mermaid Green for seat and with Brown, Whipstitch pieces together according to Study Chair Assembly Diagram on page 126.

TABLE

CUTTING INSTRUCTIONS:

NOTE: Use clear canvas throughout.

A: For top, cut one according to graph.

B: For top lip front and back, cut one 2 x 40 holes and one 2 x 24 holes (no graphs).

C: For front legs, cut two according to graph.

D: For back legs, cut one according to graph.

STITCHING INSTRUCTIONS:

1: Using colors and stitches indicated, work A, C and D pieces according to graphs. Using Brown and Continental Stitch, work B pieces.

2: With Brown, Whipstitch pieces together according to Study Table Assembly Diagram on page 125. Overcast unfinished edges.

VASE, DOILIES & CANDLESTICKS

CUTTING INSTRUCTIONS:

NOTE: Use clear canvas for A and B pieces and white canvas for C and D pieces.

A: For Vase sides, cut four according to graph.

B: For Vase bottom, cut one 6 x 6 holes (no graph).

C: For Round Doily, cut one according to graph.

D: For Half-Round Doily, cut one according to graph.

STITCHING INSTRUCTIONS:

NOTE: B, C and D pieces are unworked.

1: For Vase, using metallic cord and stitches indicated, work A pieces according to graph. Whipstitch A and B pieces together according to Vase Assembly Diagram; Overcast unfinished edges. Insert bouquet.

NOTES: Cut one end off each toothpick. For candles, melt crayon and drip over toothpicks to cover; let dry.

2: For each candlestick holder, assemble berry beads according to Candle Holder Assembly Diagram. Insert pointed end of candle into holder.

FIREPLACE GRATE & SCREEN

Substituting White/Silver for White/Gold, follow instructions for Living Room Fireplace Grate & Screen on page 118.

A – Vase Side
(cut 4)
7 x 8 holes

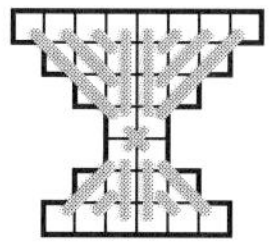

Vase Assembly Diagram

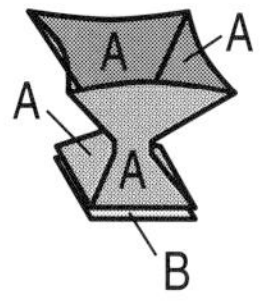

DINING ROOM COLOR KEY:

Metallic cord
- ▨ White/Silver – 10 yds.

Nylon Plus™ Needloft™ yarn

☐ #02	#00 Black	– 6 yds.
■ #36	#15 Brown	– 3 oz.
▨ #37	#53 Mermaid Green	– 24 yds.

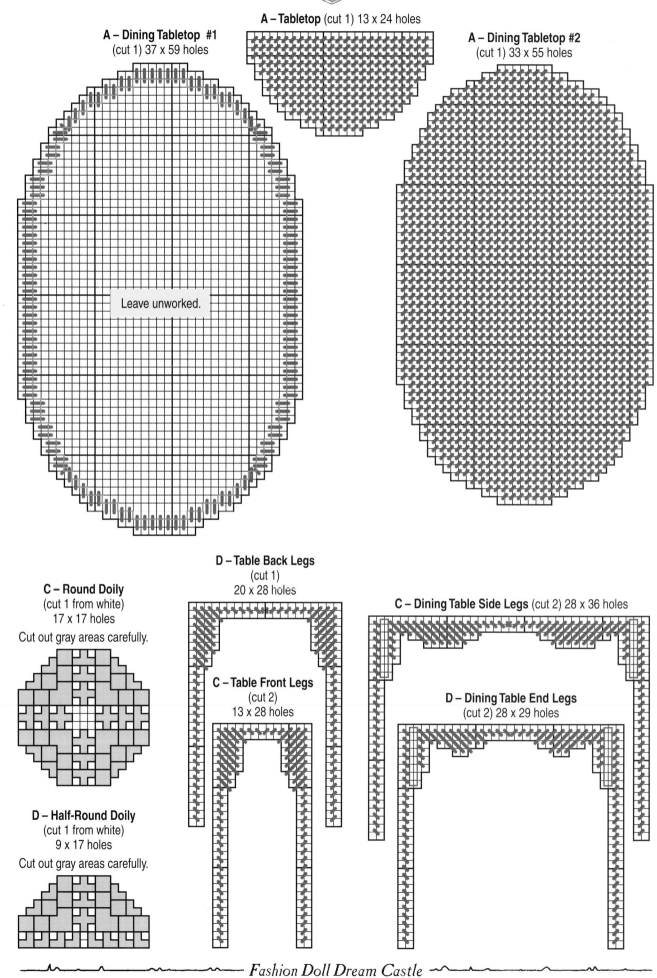

A – Tabletop (cut 1) 13 x 24 holes

A – Dining Tabletop #1
(cut 1) 37 x 59 holes

Leave unworked.

A – Dining Tabletop #2
(cut 1) 33 x 55 holes

C – Round Doily
(cut 1 from white)
17 x 17 holes

Cut out gray areas carefully.

D – Half-Round Doily
(cut 1 from white)
9 x 17 holes

Cut out gray areas carefully.

D – Table Back Legs
(cut 1)
20 x 28 holes

C – Table Front Legs
(cut 2)
13 x 28 holes

C – Dining Table Side Legs (cut 2) 28 x 36 holes

D – Dining Table End Legs
(cut 2) 28 x 29 holes

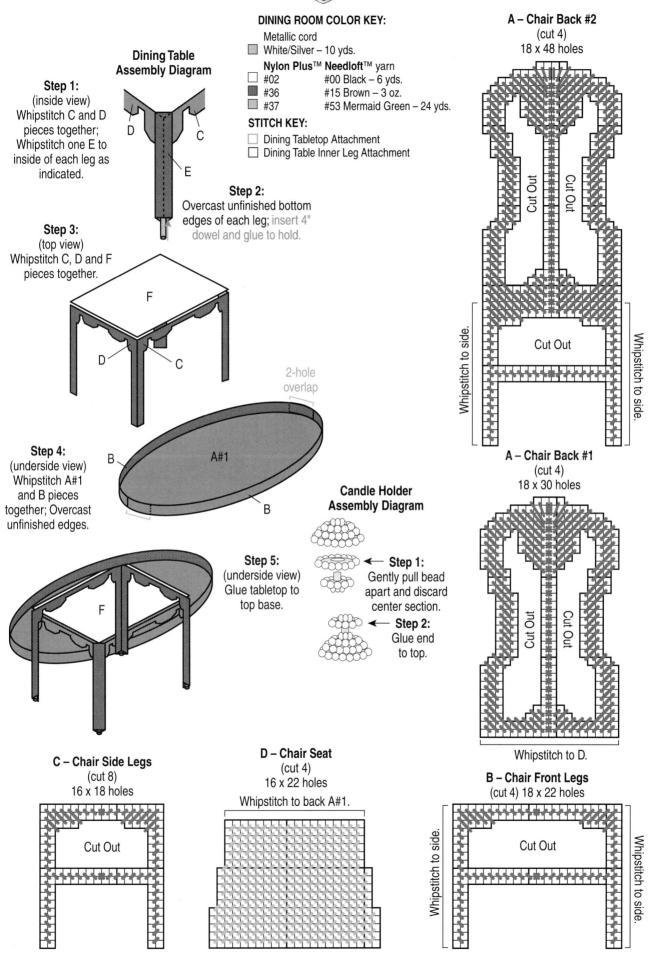

Dining Table Assembly Diagram

Step 1:
(inside view)
Whipstitch C and D pieces together; Whipstitch one E to inside of each leg as indicated.

D   C

E

Step 2:
Overcast unfinished bottom edges of each leg; insert 4" dowel and glue to hold.

Step 3:
(top view)
Whipstitch C, D and F pieces together.

F

D   C

2-hole overlap

Step 4:
(underside view)
Whipstitch A#1 and B pieces together; Overcast unfinished edges.

B   A#1   B

Step 5:
(underside view)
Glue tabletop to top base.

F

DINING ROOM COLOR KEY:

Metallic cord
White/Silver – 10 yds. #02

Nylon Plus™ Needloft™ yarn
#02   #00 Black – 6 yds.
#36   #15 Brown – 3 oz.
#37   #53 Mermaid Green – 24 yds.

STITCH KEY:
Dining Tabletop Attachment
Dining Table Inner Leg Attachment

Candle Holder Assembly Diagram

Step 1:
Gently pull bead apart and discard center section.

Step 2:
Glue end to top.

A – Chair Back #2
(cut 4)
18 x 48 holes

Cut Out   Cut Out

Cut Out

Whipstitch to side.   Whipstitch to side.

A – Chair Back #1
(cut 4)
18 x 30 holes

Cut Out   Cut Out

Whipstitch to D.

C – Chair Side Legs
(cut 8)
16 x 18 holes

Cut Out

D – Chair Seat
(cut 4)
16 x 22 holes

Whipstitch to back A#1.

B – Chair Front Legs
(cut 4) 18 x 22 holes

Cut Out

Whipstitch to side.   Whipstitch to side.

Bedroom

SIZE: Bed is 6 ¼" x 12" x 9½" tall; Vanity Table is 2½" x 4⅜" x 4⅝" tall; Vanity Stool is 1⅝" x 2½" x 3" tall; Fireplace Grate is 2" x 2½" x ¾" tall; Fireplace Screen is 1" x 3⅞" x 3⅞" tall.

MATERIALS:
☐ Two sheets of stiff 12" x 18" 7-count plastic canvas
☐ ½ sheet of black 7-count plastic canvas
☐ Scrap of white 7-count plastic canvas
☐ Three 2½"-long ⅝" wooden dowels or tree branches
☐ Brown acrylic paint (optional)
☐ 5" x 11" x 1"-thick foam rubber
☐ 5" x 10¾" x ⁵⁄₁₆"-thick Styrofoam®
☐ One 9" x 12" sheet of white felt
☐ 12" x 14" scrap of lavender cotton fabric
☐ 11" x 14" scrap of white eyelet fabric
☐ ½ yd. white 4" eyelet ruffle
☐ 1 yd. white 1¾" eyelet ruffle
☐ 1 yd. white 2" flat eyelet lace
☐ 1½ yds. lavender 1" eyelet ruffle
☐ Sewing needle or sewing machine and matching color thread
☐ Craft glue or glue gun
☐ Metallic cord; for amounts see Color Key on page 135.
☐ Worsted-weight or plastic canvas yarn; for amounts see Color Key.

NOTE: Graphs and diagrams on pages 133-135.

BED

CUTTING INSTRUCTIONS:
NOTE: Use clear canvas throughout.

A: For headboard front and back, cut one each according to graphs.

B: For headboard post pieces, cut four according to graph.

C: For top and bottom, cut one each according to graph.

D: For sides, cut two 7 x 72 holes (no graph).

E: For end, cut one 7 x 30 holes (no graph).

F: For end corners, cut two 3 x 7 holes (no graph).

G: For head end support, cut one 7 x 32 holes (no graph).

H: For center and bottom support pieces, cut four 5 x 32 holes (no graphs).

I: For dust ruffle top, using one C as a pattern, cut one from felt.

J: For bedspread top and pillow-case pieces, cut eyelet fabric according to Fabric Cutting Guide.

STITCHING INSTRUCTIONS:
NOTE: C-H pieces are unworked.

1: Using Silver metallic cord and stitches indicated, work A pieces according to graphs. For each A, overlapping one B on each side as indicated on graphs and working through both thicknesses at overlap areas as one, work B pieces (two will be worked on opposite side of canvas) according to graph.

2: With White for bed and Silver cord for headboard, assemble pieces according to Bed Assembly Diagram.

3: For dust ruffle, glue flat lace around upper edge of top C and I to top of bed.

4: For mattress, assemble foam rubber and lavender fabric according to Mattress Assembly Diagram.
NOTE: Cut one 32" and one 13" length of lavender ruffle.

5: For bedspread, press edges of bedspread eyelet fabric under ⅛". With 32" length of lavender ruffle between, sew 1¾" ruffle around side and curved end edges of fabric. Tack head end under head of mattress. For pillow, using 13" length of lavender ruffle, assemble and sew according to Pillow Assembly Diagram.

VANITY & STOOL

CUTTING INSTRUCTIONS:
NOTE: Use white canvas for H.

A: For tabletop, cut one according to graph.

B: For tabletop base, cut one according to graph.

C: For table back legs, cut one according to graph.

D: For table side legs, cut two according to graph.

E: For stool top pieces, cut one each according to graphs.

F: For stool front and back legs, cut one each according to graph.

G: For stool side legs, cut two according to graph.

H: For stool bottom, cut one according to graph.

STITCHING INSTRUCTIONS:
NOTE: B, E#2 and H pieces are unworked.

1: Using colors and stitches indicated, work A, C, D, E#1, F and G pieces according to graphs. With White, Overcast unfinished edges of A and unfinished cutout edges of C, D, F and G pieces. For table, with White and using remaining lavender ruffle, assemble pieces according to Vanity Table Assembly Diagram. Glue 4" lace around legs.

2: For stool, Whipstitch pieces together according to Vanity Stool Assembly Diagram.

FIREPLACE GRATE & SCREEN

Substituting White/Silver for White/Gold, follow instructions for Living Room Fireplace Grate & Screen on page 118.

Mattress Assembly Diagram

Step 1:
Fold lavender fabric right sides together.
12"
Fold
14"
Fold

Step 2:
Sew ½" seam.

Step 3:
Turn fabric right side out; insert foam rubber.
Seam

Step 4:
Fold in corners at ends; fold raw edges under.

Step 5:
Sew closed.
Seam

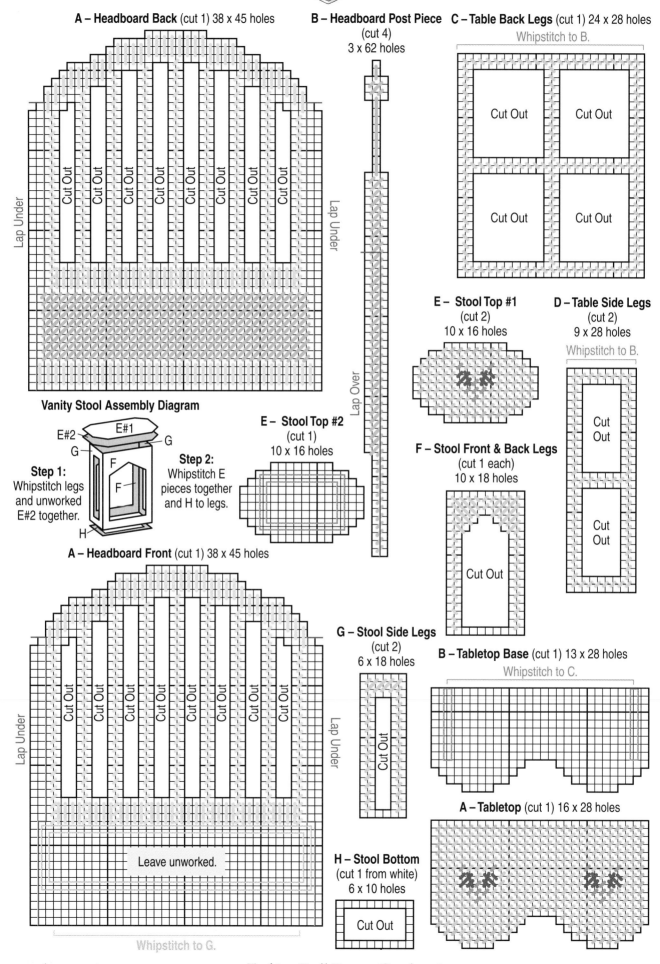

A – Headboard Back (cut 1) 38 x 45 holes

Cut Out

Lap Under

Lap Under

B – Headboard Post Piece
(cut 4)
3 x 62 holes

Lap Over

C – Table Back Legs (cut 1) 24 x 28 holes

Whipstitch to B.

Cut Out   Cut Out

Cut Out   Cut Out

E – Stool Top #1
(cut 2)
10 x 16 holes

D – Table Side Legs
(cut 2)
9 x 28 holes

Whipstitch to B.

Cut Out

E – Stool Top #2
(cut 1)
10 x 16 holes

F – Stool Front & Back Legs
(cut 1 each)
10 x 18 holes

Cut Out   Cut Out

Cut Out

Vanity Stool Assembly Diagram

E#2   E#1
G   G

Step 1:
Whipstitch legs
and unworked
E#2 together.

F
F

H

Step 2:
Whipstitch E
pieces together
and H to legs.

A – Headboard Front (cut 1) 38 x 45 holes

Cut Out

Lap Under

Lap Under

Leave unworked.

Whipstitch to G.

G – Stool Side Legs
(cut 2)
6 x 18 holes

Cut Out

H – Stool Bottom
(cut 1 from white)
6 x 10 holes

Cut Out

B – Tabletop Base (cut 1) 13 x 28 holes

Whipstitch to C.

A – Tabletop (cut 1) 16 x 28 holes

C – Top & Bottom (cut 1 each) 34 x 74 holes
Whipstitch to front A.

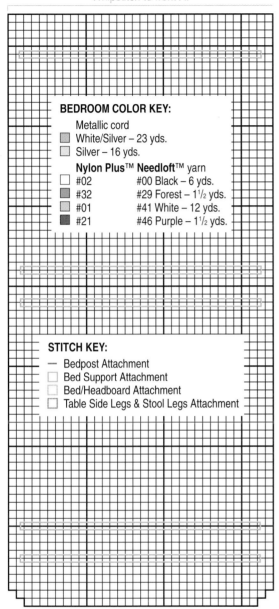

BEDROOM COLOR KEY:
Metallic cord
White/Silver – 23 yds.
Silver – 16 yds.

Nylon Plus™ Needloft™ yarn
#02   #00 Black – 6 yds.
#32   #29 Forest – 1½ yds.
#01   #41 White – 12 yds.
#21   #46 Purple – 1½ yds.

STITCH KEY:
— Bedpost Attachment
☐ Bed Support Attachment
☐ Bed/Headboard Attachment
☐ Table Side Legs & Stool Legs Attachment

J – Fabric Cutting Guide

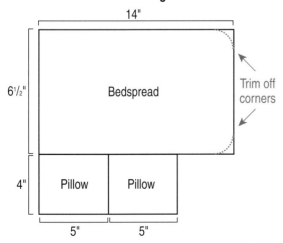

14"
6½"
Bedspread
Trim off corners
4"
Pillow   Pillow
5"   5"

Bed Assembly Diagram

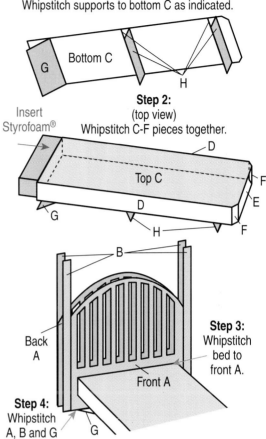

Step 1:
(underside view)
Whipstitch supports to bottom C as indicated.

Bottom C   G   H

Step 2:
(top view)
Whipstitch C-F pieces together.

Insert Styrofoam®   Top C   D   D   F   E   G   H   F

B   Back A   Front A

Step 3:
Whipstitch bed to front A.

Step 4:
Whipstitch A, B and G pieces together.   G

Vanity Table Assembly Diagram

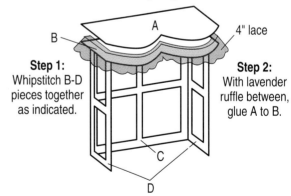

A   B   4" lace   C   D

Step 1:
Whipstitch B-D pieces together as indicated.

Step 2:
With lavender ruffle between, glue A to B.

Pillow Assembly Diagram

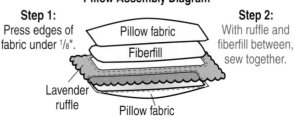

Step 1:
Press edges of fabric under ⅛".

Pillow fabric   Fiberfill   Lavender ruffle   Pillow fabric

Step 2:
With ruffle and fiberfill between, sew together.

itchen

SIZE: Sink Cabinet is 2½" x 6⅛" x 5¾" tall; Cookstove is 2⅜" x 4½" x 12½" tall.

MATERIALS:
- One sheet of stiff 12" x 18" 7-count plastic canvas
- ½ sheet of black 7-count plastic canvas
- Scrap of brown 7-count plastic canvas
- One gold 5-mm. bead
- Two red ¼" pom-poms
- 9¾" wooden ¼" dowel
- ¼" black ¾"-wide Velcro® closure
- Scraps of orange and white felt
- Two yellow ¼" paper circles or paper punch scraps
- Cookware miniatures (optional; paint with semi-flat black)
- Craft glue or glue gun
- Metallic cord; for amount see Color Key on page 139.
- Worsted-weight or plastic canvas yarn; for amounts see Color Key.

NOTE: Graphs, illustrations and diagrams on pages 138-139.

SINK CABINET

CUTTING INSTRUCTIONS:
NOTE: Use brown canvas for H.

A: For side legs, cut two according to graph.

B: For end legs, cut two according to graph.

C: For bottom shelf, cut one 16 x 40 holes.

D: For top, cut one according to graph.

E: For basin bottom, cut one according to graph.

F: For basin sides, cut two 6 x 15 holes (no graph).

G: For basin ends, cut two 6 x 12 holes (no graph).

H: For cutting board, cut one according to graph.

I: For carrots, cut four from orange felt according to Carrot Pattern.

STITCHING INSTRUCTIONS:
NOTE: H piece is unworked.

1: Using colors and stitches indicated, work A-E pieces according to graphs; Overcast unfinished cutout edges of E. Using White and Slanted Gobelin Stitch over narrow width, work F and G pieces.

2: With White for basin and with Tan, Whipstitch pieces together according to Sink Cabinet Assembly Diagram; Overcast unfinished edges.

NOTE: Cut Forest into two 9" lengths.

3: Tie cut lengths of Forest into two small bows; trim ends close to loops. For tomatoes, glue one bow to each pom-pom. For carrots, assemble according to I Pattern.

COOKSTOVE

CUTTING INSTRUCTIONS:
NOTE: Use black canvas for E, F, H and I pieces.

A: For front, cut one according to graph.

B: For sides, cut two 16 x 19 holes.

C: For front legs, cut one according to graph.

D: For side legs, cut two according to graph.

E: For base, cut two according to graphs.

F: For top, cut two according to graph.

G: For stovepipe pieces, cut four 2 x 66 holes (no graph).

H: For rack, cut one according to graph.

I: For door, cut two according to graph.

J: For egg whites, cut two from white felt according to Egg Pattern.

STITCHING INSTRUCTIONS:
NOTE: One F and H pieces are unworked.

1: Using colors and stitches indicated, work A-E, one F and I (hold door pieces together and work through both thicknesses as one) pieces according to graphs; with Black, Overcast unfinished cutout edges of A. Using Black and Continental Stitch, work G pieces.

2: With Black, Whipstitch and assemble pieces according to Cookstove Assembly Diagram. (**NOTE:** Door is not Overcast.)

3: Sew or glue closure to inside of door and corresponding area on front. For eggs, assemble according to J Pattern.

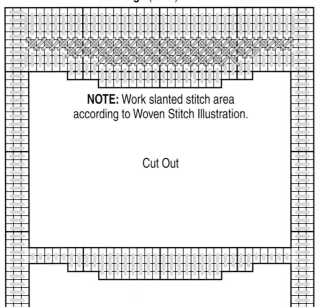

A – Side Legs (cut 2) 38 x 40 holes

NOTE: Work slanted stitch area according to Woven Stitch Illustration.

Cut Out

B – End Legs (cut 2) 16 x 38 holes

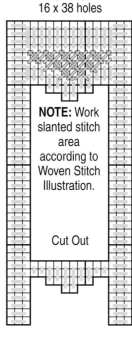

NOTE: Work slanted stitch area according to Woven Stitch Illustration.

Cut Out

E – Basin Bottom (cut 1) 12 x 15 holes

Cut out gray area.

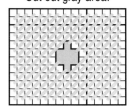

H – Cutting Board (cut 1 from brown) 9 x 15 holes

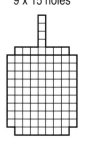

C – Bottom Shelf (cut 1) 16 x 40 holes

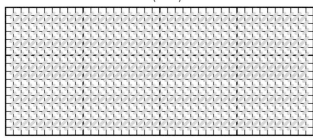

Woven Stitch Illustration

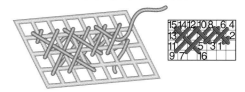

D – Top (cut 1) 16 x 40 holes

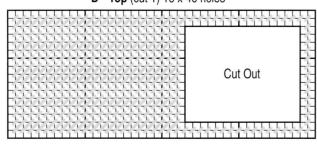

Cut Out

Sink Cabinet Assembly Diagram

Step 1: Whipstitch D-G pieces together.

Step 2: Whipstitch A-D pieces together.

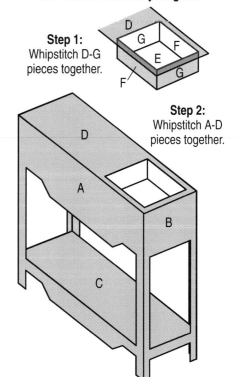

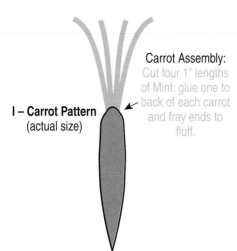

Carrot Assembly: Cut four 1" lengths of Mint; glue one to back of each carrot and fray ends to fluff.

I – Carrot Pattern (actual size)

A – Front (cut 1) 19 x 23 holes

Cut Out

Whipstitch to one E.

B – Side
(cut 2)
16 x 19 holes

E – Base
(cut 2 from black)
15 x 29 holes

Leave unworked.

F – Top
(cut 2 from black)
15 x 29 holes

Cut Out

C – Front Legs (cut 1) 13 x 23 holes

Whipstitch to one E.

D – Side Legs
(cut 2) 13 x 16 holes

Whipstitch to one E.

H – Rack
(cut 1 from black)
11 x 21 holes

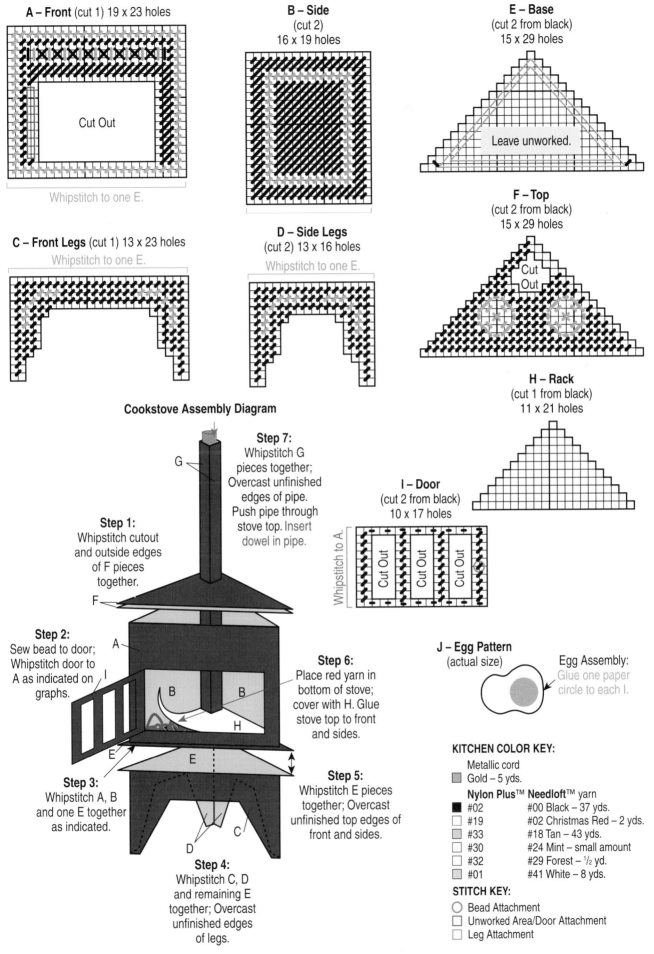

Cookstove Assembly Diagram

Step 7:
Whipstitch G pieces together; Overcast unfinished edges of pipe. Push pipe through stove top. Insert dowel in pipe.

G

Step 1:
Whipstitch cutout and outside edges of F pieces together.

F

Step 2:
Sew bead to door; Whipstitch door to A as indicated on graphs.

A

I

I – Door
(cut 2 from black)
10 x 17 holes

Whipstitch to A.

Cut Out   Cut Out   Cut Out

B   B

H

Step 6:
Place red yarn in bottom of stove; cover with H. Glue stove top to front and sides.

E

Step 3:
Whipstitch A, B and one E together as indicated.

E

Step 4:
Whipstitch C, D and remaining E together; Overcast unfinished edges of legs.

D   C

Step 5:
Whipstitch E pieces together; Overcast unfinished top edges of front and sides.

J – Egg Pattern
(actual size)

Egg Assembly:
Glue one paper circle to each I.

KITCHEN COLOR KEY:

	Metallic cord	
	Gold – 5 yds.	

Nylon Plus™ Needloft™ yarn

#02	#00 Black – 37 yds.	
#19	#02 Christmas Red – 2 yds.	
#33	#18 Tan – 43 yds.	
#30	#24 Mint – small amount	
#32	#29 Forest – 1/2 yd.	
#01	#41 White – 8 yds.	

STITCH KEY:

○ Bead Attachment
☐ Unworked Area/Door Attachment
☐ Leg Attachment

Bathroom

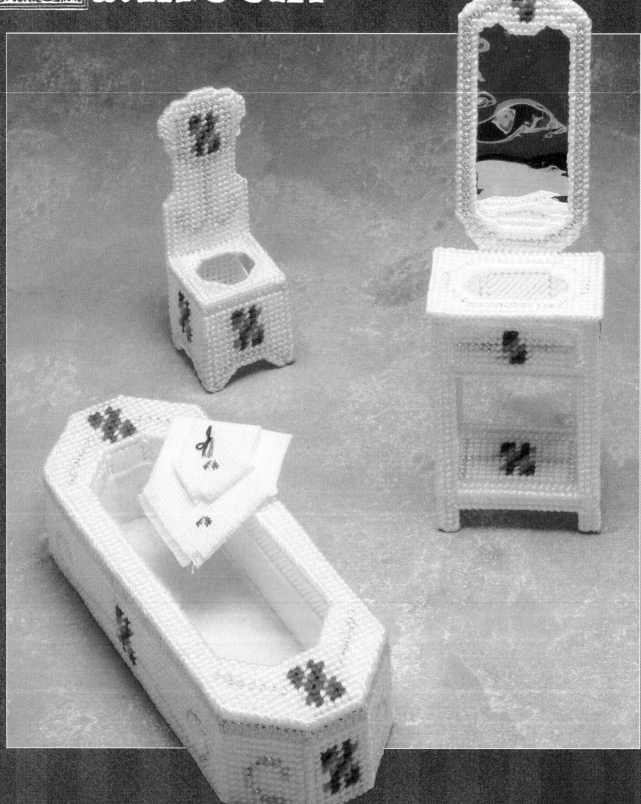

SIZE: Tub is 3¾" x 10⅝" x 2⅜" tall; Commode is 2¼" x 2¼" x 6¼" tall; Washstand is 2⅝" x 3¾" x 11¾" tall; Towels are about 3" and 5" square.

MATERIALS:
☐ Two sheets of stiff 12" x 18" 7-count plastic canvas
☐ Scraps of white 7-count plastic canvas
☐ 5" x 8" scrap of white 14-count Aida cloth
☐ One 9" x 12" sheet of white felt
☐ 2½" x 5" aluminum or craft foil
☐ Sewing needle
☐ Craft glue or glue gun
☐ Six-strand embroidery floss; for amounts see Color Key.
☐ Metallic cord; for amount see Color Key.
☐ Worsted-weight or plastic canvas yarn; for amounts see Color Key.

NOTE: Graphs, illustration and diagrams on pages 141-144.

TUB
CUTTING INSTRUCTIONS:
NOTE: Use clear canvas for A-H pieces.

A: For top, cut one according to graph.

B: For inner sides, cut two 14 x 39 holes (no graph).

C: For inner ends, cut two 6 x 14 holes (no graph).

D: For inner end corners, cut four 7 x 14 holes (no graph).

E: For bottom, cut one according to graph.

F: For outer sides, cut two 14 x 54 holes.

G: For outer ends, cut two 8 x 14 holes.

H: For outer end corners, cut four 11 x 14 holes.

I: For tub lining pieces, cut felt according to Felt Cutting Diagram.

STITCHING INSTRUCTIONS:
NOTE: E piece is unworked.

1: Using colors and stitches indicated, work A, F, G and H pieces according to graphs. Using White and Slanted Gobelin Stitch over 14-hole width, work B-D pieces.

2: With White, Whipstitch and assemble pieces according to Tub Assembly Diagram.

COMMODE
CUTTING INSTRUCTIONS:
NOTE: Use white canvas for E-G

pieces and clear canvas for remaining pieces.

A: For back pieces, cut one each according to graphs.

B: For sides and front, cut three according to graph.

C: For seat, cut one according to graph.

D: For bottom, cut one 14 x 14 holes (no graph).

E: For tray bottom, cut one 8 x 13 holes (no graph).

F: For tray sides, cut two 6 x 13 holes (no graph).

G: For tray ends, cut two 6 x 8 holes (no graph).

STITCHING INSTRUCTIONS:
NOTE: D-G pieces are unworked.

1: Using colors and stitches indicated, work A-C pieces according to graphs; with White, Overcast unfinished bottom edge of A#1 as indicated on graph and unfinished cutout edges of A#2 and C pieces.

2: With White, Whipstitch pieces together as indicated and according to Commode Assembly Diagram.

WASHSTAND
CUTTING INSTRUCTIONS:
NOTE: Use clear canvas for A-J pieces.

A: For back, cut one according to graph.

B: For mirror back, cut one according to graph.

C: For front, cut one according to graph.

D: For ends, cut two according to graph.

E: For bottom shelf, cut one 14 x 22 holes.

Half Cross Stitch Illustration

Towel Motif Graph

F: For top, cut one according to graph.

G: For sink bottom, cut one according to graph.

H: For sink sides, cut two 6 x 10 holes (no graph).

I: For sink ends and end corners, cut six 3 x 6 holes (no graph).

J: For drawer facade, cut one 6 x 18 holes.

K: For mirror backing, using B as a pattern, cut one from felt according to Felt Cutting Diagram.

STITCHING INSTRUCTIONS:
NOTE: B is unworked.

1: With White, Overcast unfinished edges of J. Using colors and stitches indicated, work A, C (hold J to C as indicated on graph and work through both thicknesses as one), D, E, F and G pieces according to graphs; Overcast unfinished mirror cutout and indicated edges of A, B and F pieces as indicated on graphs.

2: With White, Whipstitch and assemble pieces according to Washstand Assembly Diagram; Overcast unfinished edges.

TOWELS
CUTTING INSTRUCTIONS:
A: For large towel, cut one 3" x 3" piece of Aida cloth.

B: For small towel, cut one 5" x 5" piece of Aida cloth.

STITCHING INSTRUCTIONS:
1: Fray edges of A and B pieces. Using six strands floss in colors indicated and Half Cross Stitch (see Stitch Illustration), work motif according to Towel Motif Graph in one corner of each towel.

BATHROOM COLOR KEY:
Embroidery floss
■ Dk. Green – ½ yd.
■ Dk. Pink – small amount
☐ Pink – small amount
Metallic cord
☐ White/Silver – 14 yds.

Nylon Plus™ Needloft™ yarn
☐ #11   #07 Pink – 2 yds.
■ #59   #30 Avocado – 4 yds.
☐ #01   #41 White – 2½ yds.
■ #54   #55 Watermelon – 3 yds.

STITCH KEY:
✓ Half Cross Stitch

A – Tub Top (cut 1) 24 x 70 holes

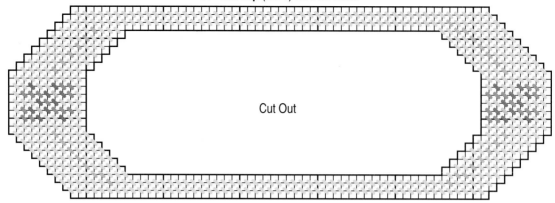

Cut Out

E – Tub Bottom (cut 1) 24 x 70 holes

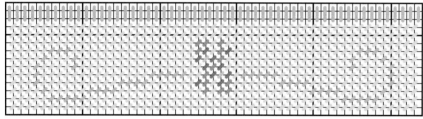

F – Tub Outer Side (cut 2) 14 x 54 holes

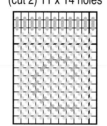

B – Washstand Mirror Back
(cut 1) 18 x 51 holes

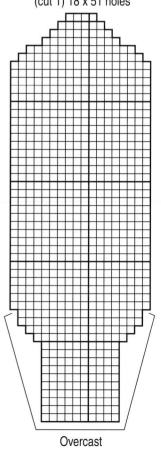

Overcast

G – Tub Outer End
(cut 2) 8 x 14 holes

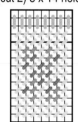

H – Tub Outer End Corner #1
(cut 2) 11 x 14 holes

H – Tub Outer End Corner #2
(cut 2) 11 x 14 holes

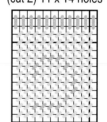

Felt Cutting Diagram

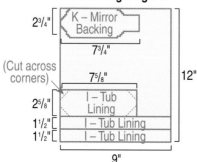

2³/₄"

K – Mirror Backing

7³/₄"

7⁵/₈"

(Cut across corners)

2⁵/₈"

I – Tub Lining

12"

1¹/₂" I – Tub Lining

1¹/₂" I – Tub Lining

9"

Commode Assembly Diagram
Step 1:
Whipstitch B-D pieces together; Overcast unfinished bottom edges.

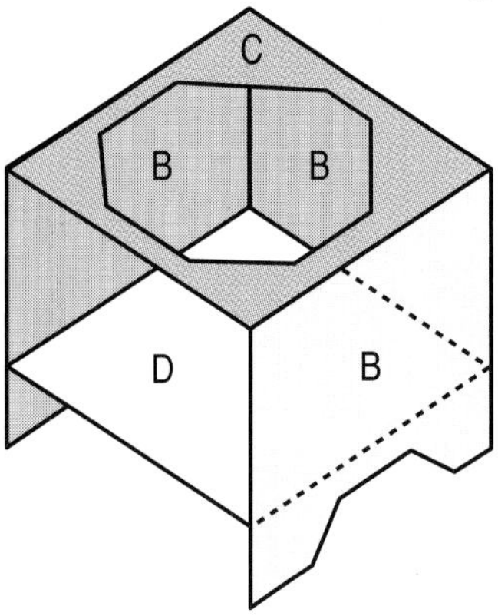

Step 2:
Whipstitch assembly and A#2 together; Whipstitch A pieces together.

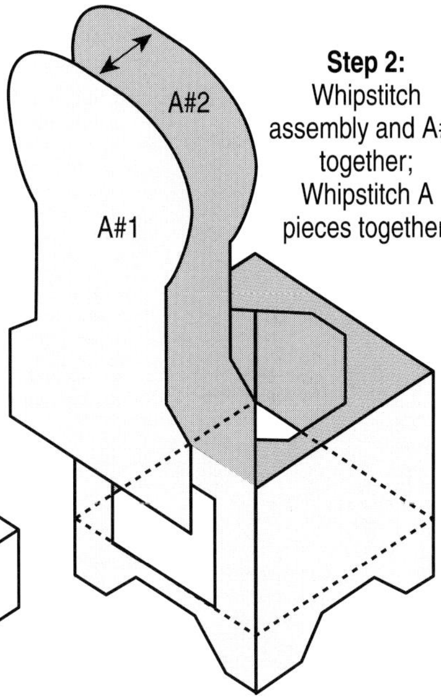

Step 3:
Whipstitch E-G pieces together, forming tray. Slide tray inside back cutout.

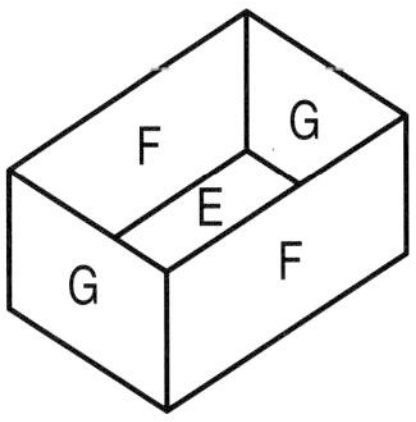

A – Commode Back #1
(cut 1) 14 x 28 holes

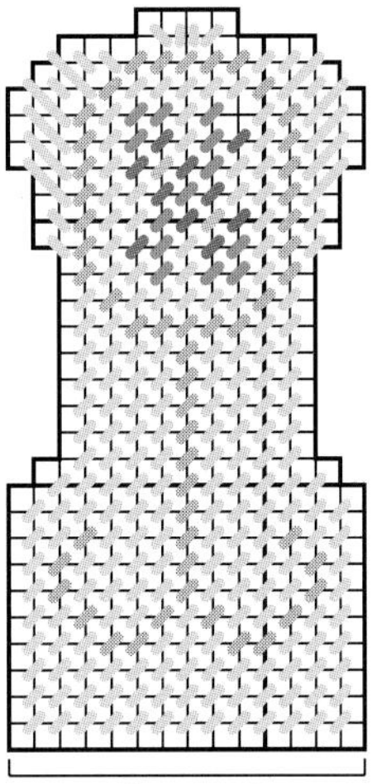

Overcast

D – Washstand End
(cut 2) 14 x 36 holes
Whipstitch to F.

Cut Out

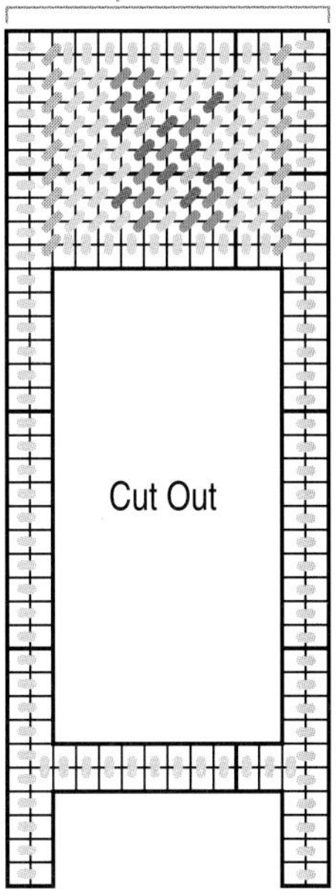

A – Commode Back #2
(cut 1) 14 x 43 holes

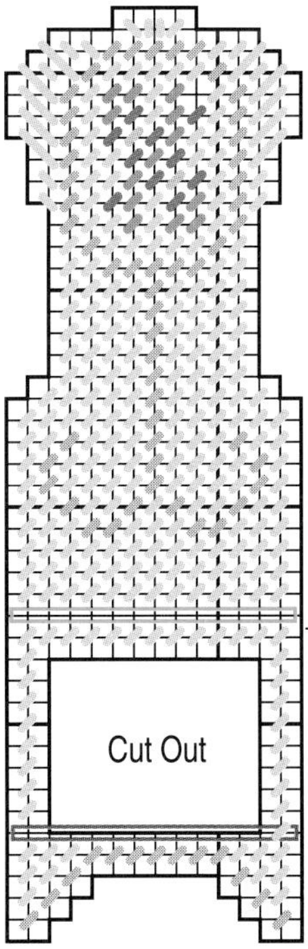

Cut Out

Work stitches below seat attachment on opposite side of canvas.

BATHROOM COLOR KEY:
Embroidery floss
Dk. Green – 1/2 yd.
Dk. Pink – small amount
Pink – small amount
Metallic cord
White/Silver – 14 yds.
Nylon Plus™ Needloft™ yarn
#11   #07 Pink – 2 yds.
#59   #30 Avocado – 4 yds.
#01   #41 White – 2½ yds.
#54   #55 Watermelon – 3 yds.

STITCH KEY:
Tub Inner Wall Attachment
Commode Seat Attachment
Do not Overcast/Commode Bottom Attachment

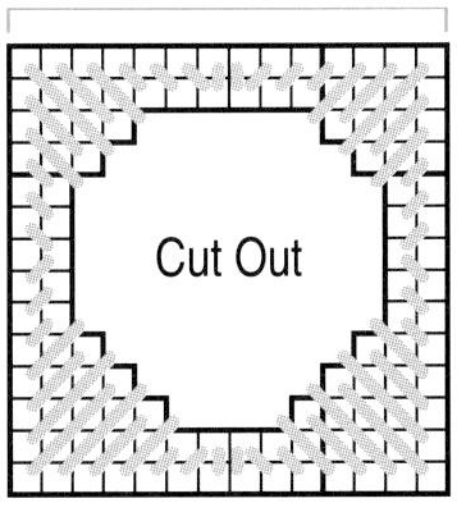

Tub Assembly Diagram
Step 1:
(underside view)
Whipstitch A-D pieces together.

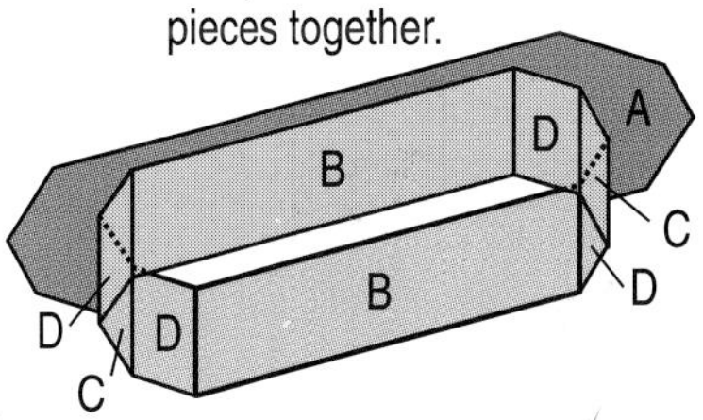

Step 2:
(top view)
Whipstitch inner walls and E together as indicated on graph.

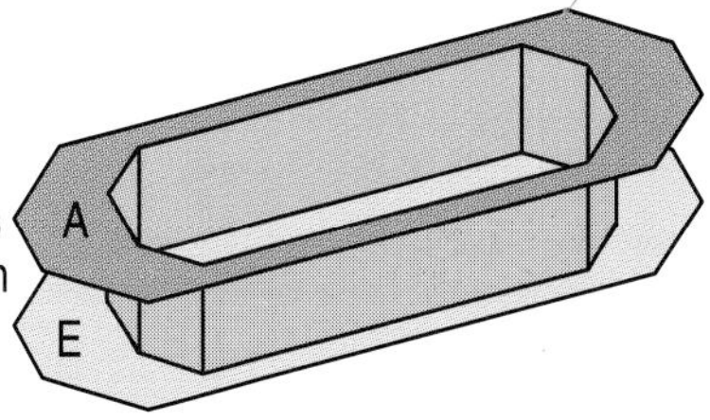

Step 3:
Whipstitch top, bottom and F-H pieces together.

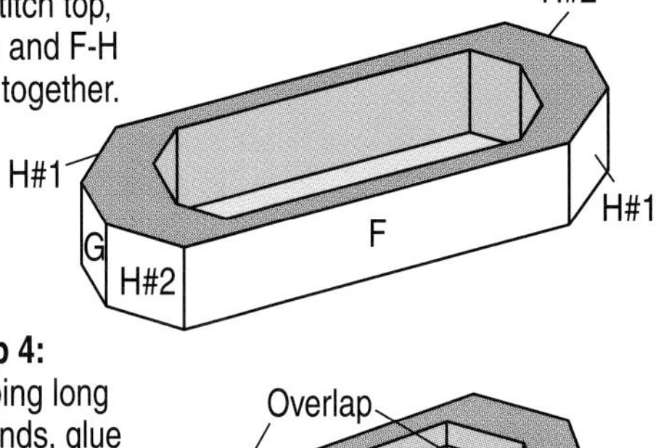

Step 4:
Overlapping long strips at ends, glue felt (I pieces) to inner walls and bottom.

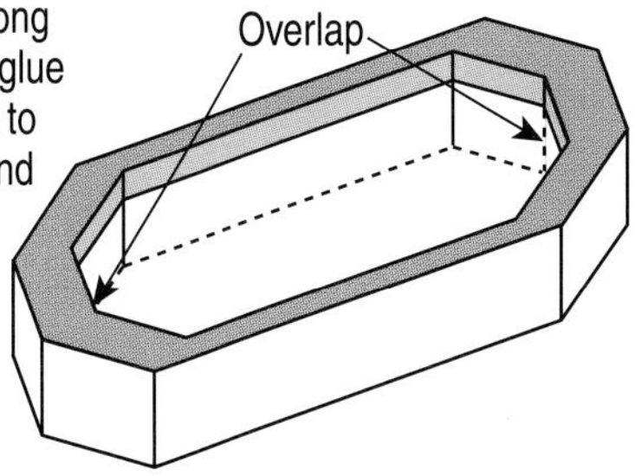

Overlap

B – Commode Side & Front
(cut 3) 14 x 15 holes

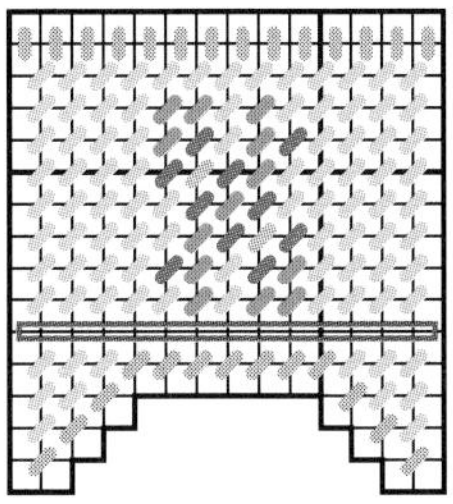

C – Commode Seat
(cut 1) 14 x 14 holes
Whipstitch to A#2.

Cut Out

A – Washstand Back
(cut 1) 22 x 78 holes

E – Washstand Bottom Shelf
(cut 1) 14 x 22 holes

C – Washstand Front
(cut 1) 22 x 36 holes

J – Washstand Drawer Facade
(cut 1) 6 x 18 holes
Whipstitch to F.

F – Washstand Top (cut 1) 15 x 24 holes
Do not Overcast; Whipstitch to A

Cut Out

Cut Out

Cut Out

Cut Out

Overcast   Overcast

Work stitches below top attachment on opposite side of canvas.

G – Washstand Sink Bottom
(cut 1) 7 x 16 holes

Cut Out

Washstand Assembly Diagram

Step 1:
(top view)
Whipstitch F-I pieces together.

Step 3:
With mirror foil between, Whipstitch unfinished edges of A and B together; glue K to back.

Step 2:
Whipstitch A and C-F pieces together as indicated.

BATHROOM COLOR KEY:
Embroidery floss
▨ Dk. Green – ½ yd.
▨ Dk. Pink – small amount
▨ Pink – small amount
Metallic cord
▨ White/Silver – 14 yds.
Nylon Plus™ Needloft™ yarn
▨ #11   #07 Pink – 2 yds.
▨ #59   #30 Avocado – 4 yds.
▨ #01   #41 White – 2½ yds.
▨ #54   #55 Watermelon – 3 yds.

STITCH KEY:
☐ Washstand Top Attachment

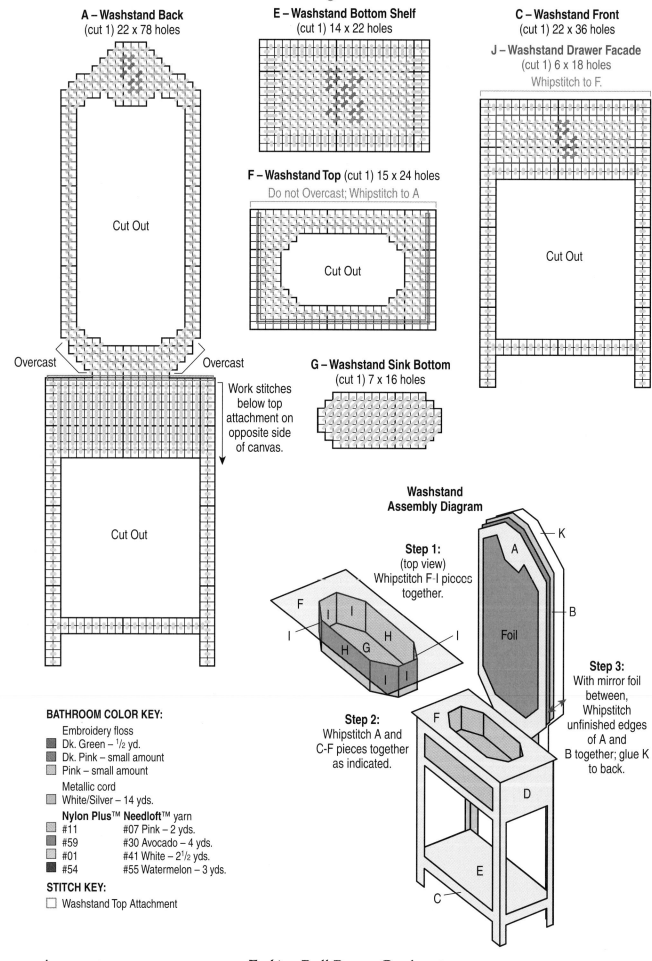

dditional Information

MATERIALS FOR ALL FURNISHINGS:
- [ ] 14 sheets of stiff 12" x 18" 7-count plastic canvas
- [ ] ½ sheet of flexible standard-size 7-count plastic canvas
- [ ] Three sheets of black 7-count plastic canvas
- [ ] One sheet of ivory 7-count plastic canvas
- [ ] ½ sheet of brown 7-count plastic canvas
- [ ] ½ sheet of white 7-count plastic canvas
- [ ] Scraps of colored 7-count plastic canvas
- [ ] One 3" and one 4¼" Crafty Circle
- [ ] 5" x 8" scrap of white 14-count Aida cloth
- [ ] Two large scalloped lace motifs
- [ ] Two sheets of white 9" x 12" felt
- [ ] Scraps of orange felt
- [ ] 12" x 14" scrap of lavender cotton fabric
- [ ] 11" x 14" scrap of white eyelet fabric
- [ ] ½ yd. white 4" eyelet ruffle
- [ ] 1 yd. white 1¾" eyelet ruffle
- [ ] 1 yd. white 2" flat eyelet lace
- [ ] 1½ yds. lavender 1" eyelet ruffle
- [ ] Four gold 3-mm. beads
- [ ] Two gold 6-mm. beads
- [ ] 36 clear and nine amber 4-mm. faceted beads
- [ ] 20⅝" clear 4-mm. prestrung pearls
- [ ] One gold 5-mm. bead
- [ ] Two white 15-mm. aurora borealis berry beads

- [ ] Two round toothpicks
- [ ] Blue crayon
- [ ] Two red ¼" pom-poms
- [ ] Ribbon rose bouquet to match Dining Room colors
- [ ] Twelve 2½"-long ⅝" wooden dowels or tree branches
- [ ] Four 4" wooden ⅛" dowels or bamboo skewers
- [ ] 9¾" wooden ¼" dowel
- [ ] Brown acrylic paint (optional)
- [ ] Two yellow ¼" paper circles or paper punch scraps
- [ ] 2½" x 5" aluminum or craft foil
- [ ] Cookware miniatures (optional; paint with semi-flat black)
- [ ] One white feather
- [ ] ½" of tan and ¼" of black ¾"-wide Velcro® closures
- [ ] 5" x 11" x 1"-thick foam rubber
- [ ] 5" x 10¾" x ⁵⁄₁₆"-thick Styrofoam®
- [ ] Polyester fiberfill
- [ ] Sewing needle or sewing machine and thread
- [ ] Craft glue or glue gun

SIX-STRAND EMBROIDERY FLOSS:
- [ ] White – 3 yds.
- [ ] Dk. Green – ½ yd.
- [ ] Dk. Pink – small amount
- [ ] Pink – small amount

METALLIC CORD:
- [ ] White/Silver – 47yds.
- [ ] White/Gold – 19 yds.
- [ ] Silver – 16 yds.
- [ ] Gold – 5½ yds.

WORSTED-WEIGHT OR PLASTIC CANVAS YARN:

Nylon Plus™	Needloft™ yarn	Nylon Plus™	Needloft™ yarn
#02	#00 Black – 61 yds.	#38	#34 Cerulean – 2 yds.
#19	#02 Christmas Red – 2 yds.	#01	#41 White – 50½ yds.
#11	#07 Pink – 2 yds.	#34	#43 Camel – 3½ oz.
#36	#15 Brown – 5 oz.	#21	#46 Purple – 1½ yds.
#33	#18 Tan – 43 yds.	#08	#50 Teal Blue – 2 yds.
#30	#24 Mint – 3 oz.	#37	#53 Mermaid Green – 24 yds.
#32	#29 Forest – 2 yds.	#54	#55 Watermelon – 3 yds.
#59	#30 Avocado – 4 yds.		

MATERIALS FOR CASTLE AND FURNISHINGS:

- [ ] 110 sheets of stiff 12" x 18" 7-count plastic canvas
- [ ] Two sheets of standard-size (regular flexibility) 7-count plastic canvas
- [ ] ½ sheet of flexible standard-size 7-count plastic canvas
- [ ] Three sheets of black 7-count plastic canvas
- [ ] One sheet of ivory 7-count plastic canvas
- [ ] ½ sheet of brown 7-count plastic canvas
- [ ] ½ sheet of white 7-count plastic canvas
- [ ] Scraps of colored 7-count plastic canvas
- [ ] One 3" and one 4¼" Crafty Circle
- [ ] 5" x 8" scrap of white 14-count Aida cloth
- [ ] Two large scalloped lace motifs
- [ ] 1½ yds. white 30"-wide felt
- [ ] Two sheets of white 9" x 12" felt
- [ ] Scraps of orange felt
- [ ] 12" x 14" scrap of lavender cotton fabric
- [ ] 1½ yds. lavender 1" eyelet ruffle
- [ ] 11" x 14" scrap of white eyelet fabric
- [ ] ½ yd. white 4" eyelet ruffle
- [ ] 1 yd. white 1¾" eyelet ruffle
- [ ] 1⅛ yds. white 7"-wide lace
- [ ] 1 yd. white 2" flat eyelet lace
- [ ] 12" each of 1½"-wide lt. and dk. teal heavy satin ribbon
- [ ] 36 clear and nine amber 4-mm. faceted beads
- [ ] 20⅝" clear 4-mm. prestrung pearls
- [ ] 36 gold 3-mm. beads
- [ ] 14 gold 5-mm. beads
- [ ] Two gold 6-mm. beads
- [ ] 42 silver 3-mm. beads
- [ ] 37 silver 4-mm. beads
- [ ] Seven white 15-mm. aurora borealis berry beads
- [ ] 12" of prestrung clear aurora borealis beads
- [ ] 18 blue 5-mm. faceted beads
- [ ] Two round toothpicks
- [ ] Blue crayon
- [ ] Two red ¼" pom-poms
- [ ] Ribbon rose bouquet
- [ ] Twelve 2½"-long ⅝" wooden dowels or tree branches
- [ ] 45" wooden ⅛" dowel
- [ ] Four 4" wooden ⅛" dowels or bamboo skewers
- [ ] 9¾" wooden ¼" dowel
- [ ] Two 12¾" wooden ½" dowels (optional; paint white)
- [ ] 6¼" heavy gauge floral or clothes hanger wire
- [ ] Brown acrylic paint (optional)
- [ ] Silver acrylic paint
- [ ] Silver glitter fabric paint
- [ ] Two yellow ¼" paper circles or paper punch scraps
- [ ] Pictures from magazines or encyclopedias
- [ ] One 2½" x 3½" and two 2½" x 5" pieces of aluminum or craft foil
- [ ] Two 1½"-wide lion's head drawer pulls
- [ ] One two-hole drawer pull backplate with 3" between holes (backplate in photo is 1⅛" x 5½")
- [ ] Two ½"-long No. 8 brass screws with nuts (32 threads per inch)
- [ ] Cookware miniatures (optional; paint with semi-flat black)
- [ ] One white feather
- [ ] 16" of white, 2½" of tan and ¼" of black ¾"-wide Velcro® closures
- [ ] 5" x 11" x 1"-thick foam rubber
- [ ] 5" x 10¾" x 5⁄16"-thick Styrofoam®
- [ ] Polyester fiberfill
- [ ] Sewing needle or machine and thread
- [ ] Craft glue or glue gun

SIX-STRAND EMBROIDERY FLOSS:

- [ ] White – 3 yds.
- [ ] Dk. Green – ½ yd.
- [ ] Gray – ½ yd.
- [ ] Dk. Pink – small amount
- [ ] Pink – small amount

METALLIC CORD:

- [ ] White/Silver – 177 yds.
- [ ] White/Gold – 116 yds.
- [ ] Silver – 16 yds.
- [ ] Gold – 5½ yds.

WORSTED-WEIGHT OR PLASTIC CANVAS YARN:

Nylon Plus™	Needloft™ yarn	Nylon Plus™	Needloft™ yarn
#02	#00 Black – 6 oz.	#23	#38 Gray – 35 oz.
#19	#02 Christmas Red – 2 yds.	#24	#39 Eggshell – 4 oz.
#11	#07 Pink – 62 yds.	#01	#41 White – 2½ oz.
#35	#13 Maple – 16½ oz.	#34	#43 Camel – 5 oz.
#36	#15 Brown – 5 oz.	#22	#45 Lilac – 2½ oz.
#27	#17 Gold – 3½ oz.	#21	#46 Purple – 7½ yds.
#33	#18 Tan – 2½ oz.	#46	#47 Peach – 3½ oz.
#42	#21 Baby Yellow – 42 yds.	#08	#50 Teal Blue – 30 yds.
#30	#24 Mint – 3½ oz.	#60	#51 Aqua – 3 oz.
#28	#26 Baby Green – 2½ oz.	#37	#53 Mermaid Green – 24 yds.
#32	#29 Forest – 8 yds.	#54	#55 Watermelon – 5 yds.
#59	#30 Avocado – 15 yds.	#26	#57 Yellow – small amount
#38	#34 Cerulean – 25 yds.		